A Brief History

of the

Saugeen Peninsula

David D Plain

 www.trafford.com

North America & international
toll-free: 1 888 232 4444 (USA & Canada)
fax: 812 355 4082

Contents

CULTURE

APPENDICES

Other Books by David D Plain

The Plains of Aamjiwnaang
Ways of Our Grandfathers
1300 Moons
From Ouisconsin to Caughnawaga
Poems from an Eclectic Mind

Dedicated to

MY GRANDFATHER, JOSEPH ROOT, A WORLD WAR I ANISHNAABEK WARRIOR FROM SAUGEEN OJIBWAY NATION.

Preface

I have written the brief history on the Saugeen Ojibwa in honour of my grandparents Eleanor and Joseph Root. They were members of the Saugeen Ojibwa Nation. I am a member of the Aamjiwnaang First Nation. Nicholas Plain, my father, was an elected chief of Aamjiwnaang, his father, Zaagmshkodewe (On the Plain), was the last traditional chief. His father, Mesquahewegezhigk (Red Sky) was a war chief from Aamjiwnaang. His father, Animikince (Little Thunder) was also a war chief as was his father, Kioscance (Little Gull).

I have a Master Degree in Theology from Tyndale Seminary, Toronto. I had a double major theology and church history. My thesis was on Biblical interpretation using indigenous thought patterns, which were arrived at using cultural anthropology as a springboard. This entailed an in-depth study of Ojibwa history and culture, which was further honed writing four books, three non-fiction and one historical fiction, on the history of the Ojibwa covering a 250-year period. I have spent many hours studying first-hand accounts and source documents as well as listening to oral history as told by the elders. This, as well as research methodologies learned along the way to a graduate level education, has qualified me to act as an aboriginal historian.

This book, as can be seen by its title, is only a brief overview of Saugeen history and culture and is by no means exhaustive. The historical section will only highlight significant life-changing events. The cultural section will give an overview of major traditions and customs in order to preview Saugeen lifestyle during the traditional period (1700-1900 C.E.).

History

CHAPTER 1

Early History

Various First Nations people have occupied Saugeen Territory for millennia. The archaeological record confirms this as the following concise summary of Bruce County illustrates:

The Middle Woodland cultures were hunters and gatherers who lived in the area from about 700 B.C. to 800 A.D. and three of their communities have been found. The Inverhuron site (~16 km south of the mouth of the Saugeen River) on the Lake Huron shore was excavated in 1972. The Donaldson site at Lot 57, Indian Strip, Amabel Township (~3 km up the Saugeen River) was excavated in 1971. The Thede site, Lot 12, Concession 8, Saugeen Township (~16 km upstream on the west side of the Saugeen River) was excavated in 1969/70.

Later in the 14th century in Saugeen Township, at Port Elgin, there was a large Iroquois village, which had double palisades and twelve longhouses. It is believed about 500 people lived here and archaeologists are not sure why they abandoned it. They were ancestors of the Huron-Petun (Tobacco Nation) people. The nearest contemporary Iroquois village was about 80 miles to the east in Simcoe County. The Port Elgin site was believed to be a trading post with the Algonquian speaking peoples to the north. There were many copper artefacts and some ceramics found at this site that certainly came from the north.

To the south at the Inverhuron site, there is evidence of earlier occupation by First Nations from the Michigan side of the lake. Perhaps the presence of the Iroquois put the area in conflict over fishing and hunting.

The Huron nation was in the area when the first French explorers and Jesuit priests arrived ... Who was the first European in Bruce County? One can only speculate that perhaps it was the French explorer, Samuel de Champlain, who arrived in 1619 at the village where the present-day city of Owen Sound is located in Grey County. Or perhaps one of the Jesuit missionaries that visited the village at the mouth of the Saugeen River, present-day Southampton. [Note: a small silver Cross of Lorraine was found at Southampton in 1909, probably from the Jesuits, and is presently housed in the Bruce County Museum.]

An early Jesuit map, dated 1656, shows a Jesuit mission called St. Peter and St. Paul, located somewhere in the southern end of Bruce County. The main Jesuit mission, at Huronia near present-day Midland, was overrun by invading Iroquois from the south in March of 1649. The Jesuits (Father Brébeuf) were martyred and the Hurons were forced to abandon the area. The Iroquois then used the region as their hunting ground.

After the mid-1600s the Ojibway, later known as the Chippewas, from the Lake Superior area, sent trading parties to Montreal to trade fur. The Iroquois frequently killed these trading parties and so the Ojibway and their allies retaliated and forced the Iroquois (Mohawk) out. The Ojibway held the area for the next several generations[1]

---

1 Bruce County Genealogical Society, History, http://www.rootsweb. com/%7Eonbcgs/bcgshist.htm; Internet; accessed 16 June 2005.

CHAPTER 2

Iroquois War in Saugeen Territory

This retaliation happened at the end of the seventeenth century when the Three Fires Confederacy (Ojibwa, Odawah, and Potawatomi) with the other Algonquin allies as well as the Wyandotte went on the offensive against the Five Nations (Iroquois). Two of the five nations, the Senecas and Mohawks, were using Southern Ontario as hunting and trapping territories. A peace council between the Three Fires and Five Nations Confederacy held earlier at the mouth of the Saugeen River had failed. According to George Copway, the Mohawks held the peace for a short time but soon returned to their old ways of waylaying Ojibwa traders on their way to Montreal killing them and stealing their goods.[2] War was determined as the only solution to the "Iroquois problem". The following are where the battles were fought in Saugeen Territory.

Battle of Skull Mound

The major War Chief that led this battle was Kioscance who was a Bawitigwakinini Ojibwa from the Sault Ste. Marie area. He first led his forces to Lake St. Clair where he annihilated a large Seneca town

---

2 For Copway's account of the Iroquois War see Copway, G. *The Traditional History and Characteristics of the Ojibway Nation*, Charles Gilpin, London: 1850, 77-94.

on the River Thames. George Copway's account agrees with Governor Denonville's observation that before the Ojibwa moved up the Lake Huron coast to Saugeen they gathered at St. Clair.[3] "It is related that Kioscance was chief of the Otchipwes in their wars against the Wyandots and Six Nations. In his expedition from Lake Superior to Lake Erie, his fleet was so extensive as to cover the St. Clair River from Fort St. Joseph, or Gratiot, to Walpole Island. On his return from the lower lakes, he camped at Fort Gratiot, and afterward made the district his home."[4]

He then moved north up Lake Huron to the mouth of the Saugeen River. This is where the Battle of Skull Mound against the Mohawks was fought. "Tradition informs us that seven hundred canoes met at Kewetawahonning ... one party was to take the route toward the river St. Clair and meet the southern Hurons ... Those who had gone to St. Clair had likewise a fierce battle at the mouth of a river called by the Algonquin Sahgeeng".[5]

The artist Paul Kane visited Saugeen in 1845 to do some sketches. He wrote in his journal the following observance of the remains of the Battle of Skull Mound, "The Indian village of Saugeen, meaning 'the mouth of a river' contains about 200 inhabitants (Ojibbeways). It is the site of a former battleground between the Ojibbeways, as usually pronounced, or Ojibwas, and the Mohawks. Of this, the mounds erected over the slain afford abundant evidence in the protrusion of bones through the surface of the ground.[6]

---

3 Schmalz, Peter. *The Ojibwa of Southern Ontario*, University of Toronto Press, Toronto: 1991, 22.

4 History of St. Clair County, Michigan, Illustrated, A.T. Andreas Co. Chicago: 1883, 608.

5 Copway, *Traditional History*, 87-88.

6 Kane, Paul. *Wanderings of an Artist Among the Indians of North America*, Longman, Brown, Green, Longmans and Roberts, London: 1859, 3.

CHAPTER 3

Other Battles of the Iroquois War in Saugeen Territory

"According to the oral tradition of the two reserves in the Saugeen area, Cape Croker and Chippewa Hill, there were numerous confrontations in their territory. In the weeks following the Battle of Skull Mound, their tradition indicates that battles occurred inland, along the shore and on the islands of Georgian Bay and Lake Huron in the vicinity of the Saugeen (Bruce) Peninsula. The Iroquois lost in a conflict on the clay banks (in Walkerton), on Indian Hill near the Teeswater River, and at Wadi-weediwon (Owen Sound). Three hundred warriors were defeated in an entrenched position on the northwest side of White Cloud Island in Colpoy Bay, the island taking its name from the victorious Ojibwa chief. Moreover, weapons of war have been found a few miles away on Griffith Island and at Cabot's head, where tradition indicates another victory occurred. In the Fishing Islands, north of the mouth of the Saugeen River, Red Bay received its name from the condition of the water after the Mohawk were defeated there. Skull Island in the Georgian Bay was also given its name from the remains of the vanquished. Kahkewaquonaby (Peter Jones) in his History of the Ojibway Indians wrote in 1864: There they fell on a large body of the Naudoways (Iroquois) who had been dancing and feasting for several nights, and were so exhausted as to have sunk into a profound sleep the night on which they were killed. The island is called Pequahkoondebaymenis, that is, Skull Island, from the number of skulls left on it."[7]

Oral tradition comes from interviews with chiefs, band councillors, and other leading members of the communities of Saugeen and Cape Croker reserves in the period 1968-89. The informants are from the major families on the reserves, including the Joneses, Akiwenzies, Masons, Johnstons, Elliotts, Nadjiwons, Kahgees, and Kewageshigs. Local archaeologist Fritz Knechtel was also most helpful. See also Rose M. MacLeod, The Story of White Cloud, Hay and Griffith Islands (Owen Sound, Ont. 1979), 4; and the Wiarton Echo, 3 August 1883, which indicates that a great battle against the Mohawk was conducted at Cabot's Head. The battle on Indian Hill, Lot 22 Concession 15 of Culross Township, is recorded in Marion McGillivary, ed., All Our Yesterdays: A History of Culross Township, 1854-1984 (Owen Sound, Ont. 1984), 20. Many of these accounts are traditions of the farming community passed on from the early pioneers who received them from the local Indians; see Smith, 'Who are the Mississauga?' 'The Mississauga, Peter Jones and the White Man'; Jones, History, 112. The location of Skull Island is not specifically given by Jones; however, James White in 'Place Names in Georgian Bay,' Ontario Historical Society, Papers and Records 11 (1913): 70, identifies one location as Skull Island where 'a large number of skeletons were found in a pit in the rock on the island.'"[8]

These are the battles that were fought in Saugeen Territory but the Iroquois War was much wider in scope. It was fought in the whole of Southern Ontario and also in upstate New York. Two of the major chiefs of the Five Nations approached the Governor of New York, to ask for assistance from their British Allies. They explained to the Governor "But they [Iroquois] are fully & firmly determined, to hold fast on the Covenant Chain made with the English, & that if the Great King of England will defend them against the Dowagenhaws the Twich Twees & other Nations over whom the French have an Influence & who have murdered several of their People since the Peace, They will have no further Correspondance with the French."[9]

---

7 Schmalz, *Ojibwa*, 23-24.

8 Ibid. 272.

9 Wraxall, Peter in: *Harvard Historical Studies*, vol. XXI, 33-34.

The following is the Governor's answer:

"Albany 29 August 1700-

The Earl of Bellomont had a Private Conference with Two of the principal Sachems of each of the 5 Nations wherein he told them.

You must needs be sensible that the Dowagenhaws, Twichtwees, Ottowawas & Diondedees and the other Remote Indians are vastly more numerous than you 5 Nations, and that by their continual Warring upon you they will in a few years totally destroy you; I should, therefore, think it prudent & good Policy in you to try all possible Means to fix a Trade & Correspondance with all those Nations, by which means you would retain them to yourselves, and with my Assistance I am in hopes in a short time they might be brought to be united with us in the Covenant Chain, and then you might be brought to be united with us in the Covenant Chain, and then you might at all times go a hunting into their Country without any sort of hazard which I understand is much the best for Bever hunting.

I wish you would try to bring some of them to speak with me, perhaps I might prevail with them to come & live amongst you and I should think myself obliged to reward you for such a piece of Service... They pray that there may be a good regulation of the Trade & Goods sold Cheap that the Remote Indians may see what Pennyworths there is here which will draw them hither."[10]

As can be seen by his answer the British were in no position to be of any assistance in the war and were really interested more in trade than helping their First Nation allies. As a result, the Five Nations were driven

10 Ibid. 34, 35, 37.

from Southern Ontario, that left this huge territory empty, and the spoils of war.

Different groups of Ojibwa moved into these new hunting and trapping grounds. The Bawitigwakinini Ojibwa moved into South-western Ontario and Southeastern Michigan. The French called this Ojibwa band Sauteurs (People of the Falls) from the word Saut meaning falls or rapids. This appellation is natural given the Huron name for them, "Eskiaeronnon-'people of the Skia,e' ("falls")"[11] and the Dakota appellation "Ra-ra-to-oans (People of the Falls).[12] The Mississauga (Eagle gens) Ojibwa located in Central and South-eastern Ontario and it was most likely the Amikwa (Beaver gens) Ojibwa who moved into the territories south of Georgian Bay probably under the leadership of White Cloud one of the principal Ojibwa War Chiefs during the Iroquois War. White Cloud Island off the Bruce Peninsula on the Georgian Bay side is named after him because of a great victory he won over the Mohawks there. These southern Georgian Bay territories included the Saugeen territory. The Ojibwa continued to live a traditional life of hunting, fishing and gathering in their new territories until the land surrenders and reserve period of the nineteenth century. These appellations to the Ojibwa Nation will be dealt with in more detail in the sections on Band Designations and Totems.

---

11 Kinietz, W. Vernon, *The Indians of the Western Great Lakes 1615-1760*, Ann Arbor Paperbacks, University of Michigan Press, 1991 318.

12 Warren, William W. *History of the Ojibway People*, Minnesota Historical Society Press, St. Paul: 1984, 96.

CHAPTER 4

War of 1812

Ojibwa First Nations at Manitoulin Island, Coldwater and Saugeen were known at this time as Lake Huron Indians. Assikenack or Blackbird, an Ojibwa Chief from Manitoulin "possibly took part in the capture of Michilimakinac in 1812 ... he commanded the Indian forced that attacked the column abandoning Fort Dearborn [Chicago] August 15, 1812, and accepted the surrender of the U.S. commander, Captain Heald".[13] Musquakie or Yellowhead principle chief of Lake Simcoe was "severely wounded in defence of York [Toronto] in 1813."[14] Warriors from Saugeen Territory also fought in the War of 1812. They fought as allies of the British against the Americans. One of their most famous war chiefs was Naiwash who was born at Saugeen and fought with Tecumseh at McGregor's Creek, October 3, 1813, and at the Battle of Moravian Town [Fairfield], October 5, 1813.[15] He would have undoubtedly fought at Detroit, Frenchtown and Fort Meigs as well. The Americans, civilians and military alike dreaded Tecumseh's Indian Confederacy. The following description of his warriors was described by Major Richardson, of the 41st Regiment on their way to Frenchtown in January 1813:

No other sound than the measured step of the troops interrupted the solitude of the scene, rendered more imposing by the appearance of the warriors, whose bodies, stained and painted in the most frightful

---

13 Curnoe, Greg. *Deeds/Nations*, eds. Frank Davey and Neal Ferris, London Chapter OAS Occasional Publication #4, 1996,8-9.

14 Schmalz, *Ojibwa*, 114.

15 Curnoe, *Deeds/Nations*, 78.

manner for the occasion, glided by us with almost noiseless velocity; some painted white, some black, others half black and half red, half black and half white; all with their hair plastered in such a way as to resemble the bristling quills of the porcupine, with no other covering than a cloth around their loins, yet armed to the teeth with rifles, tomahawks, war clubs, spears, bows and arrows, and scalping knives. Uttering no sound, and intent on reaching the enemy unperceived ...

Colonel Proctor says, in his dispatch to Sir G. Provost, "After suffering, for our numbers, a considerable loss, the enemy's force posted in the houses and enclosures, which from dread of falling into the hands of the Indians, they most obstinately defended, at length surrendered at discretion; the other part of their force in attempting to retreat by the way they came, were, I believe, all, or with very few exceptions, killed by the Indians."[16]

Proctor had refused to make a stand at Malden and retreated up the Thames River when the American forces advanced across the border. Two days before the Battle of Moravian town the Indian Confederacy tested the Americans at McGregor's Creek in order to delay their advance. Naiwash participated along with other chiefs and fifteen hundred warriors. The American general, Harrison, brought more than three thousand men up the Thames. The warriors tried to destroy the bridges that spanned the creek. They succeeded in burning the upper bridge, about a mile from the mouth of the creek but the larger one at the mouth was too wet to burn. They had to be satisfied by just pulling up the planks of the bridge. There was a skirmish that lasted about two hours and then the Indian lines broke. Tecumseh was wounded in the arm and many of his confederates scattered. The next day only five hundred formed their battle lines.[17]

Naiwash was second in command under Tecumseh at the Battle of the Moravian town. Proctor fled as soon as the encounter began. "Five minutes after the first shock Proctor's troops were flying in all directions. We are told that the General, without making an attempt to rally his men, fled in his carriage, hotly pursued by the enemy..."[18] Tecumseh's

---

16 Edgar, Matilda, *Ten Years of Upper Canada in Peace and War, 1805-1815; being The Ridout Letters*, William Briggs, Toronto: 1890 174.

17 Sugden, John, *Tecumseh*, Henry Holt and Company, New York: 1997, 366.

18 Edgar, *Ten Years*, 232.

forces were under attack from Richard Mentor Johnson's regiment of one thousand mounted Kentucky volunteers. "They waited until the enemy was within a few paces of them, and then hurled on them a deadly shower of bullets. In this part of the field, the undergrowth was so thick that the mounted riflemen could not advance. They were therefore ordered to carry on the fight on foot ... For a while, victory hung in the balance, but at last the great leader, Tecumseh, fell, and then his followers gave way and scattered through the woods."[19] This event effectively broke the Pan Indian Confederacy and although some continued to fight on they were irregular and unorganized. Naiwash complained in October 1814, "We Indians ... from the westward, perhaps the Master of Life would give us more luck if we would stick together as we formerly did ... and we probably might go back and tread again upon our own lands. Chiefs and warriors, since our great chief Tecumtha has been killed we do not listen to one another. We do not rise together. We hurt ourselves by it. It is our own fault ... We do not, when we go to war, rise together, but we go one or two, and the rest say they will go tomorrow."[20]

The War of 1812 was the last time the Ojibwa were looked upon as allies. The war opened the door for a new relationship with the British and the era of land surrenders and the creation of the reserve system.

---

19 Ibid. 233.

20 Sugden, *Tecumseh*, 384.

CHAPTER 5

Missionaries and the Colonial Government

After the American Revolution European society was quickly becoming the dominant society in Southern Ontario. Many United Empire Loyalists immigrated to Upper Canada after the Revolutionary War. The floodgates opened after the defeat of Napoleon in 1815 with tens of thousands of people, mostly from Great Britain, immigrating to Upper Canada. "From 1815 to 1824 the non-Aboriginal population doubled, from 75 000 to 150 000, mainly as a result of heavy immigration from Britain."[21] This caused a great need for farmland so the British Colonial Government began to coerce First Nations into surrendering large tracts of land to fill this need reserving small tracts of land for the First Nations. To accommodate this need the Government concluded six major land-surrender treaties that saw over 3 million hectares of Ojibwa land change hands.

The government and the church hoped for total assimilation. They wanted First Nations people to become 'Europeanized' farming for cash crops. This did not happen. Instead, First Nations only adjusted their lifestyle from large hunting territories to small reserves of land. Rather than farming for cash crops, they farmed for the needs of the community only. This replaced hunting as a major source of food. Other activities such as fishing and sugar making remained the same. This was extremely

---

21 Surtees, Robert J. "Land Cessions, 1763-1830," in *Aboriginal Ontario*, ed. Edward S. Rogers and Donald B. Smith (Toronto: Dundurn Press, 1994), 112.

frustrating to both the government and the missions as can be readily seen by the reports filed by the agent and the missionary for Saugeen in 1858. (See Appendix 1)

Before any cessions of Saugeen lands, the main village of the Saugeen Ojibwa was located at the mouth of the Saugeen River on Lake Huron. There was also a village called Nawash located at the current site of Owen Sound. According to the Indian Agent's report of 1858 (Appendix 1) the Saugeen Ojibwa split into two distinct bands after the Treaty of 1836, but there is an "Indian Settlement" located on a 1788 map at present-day Owen Sound (See Appendix 4). However, they do not appear on a "Census of the Indian Tribes" of 1736[22] nor do they appear on the ca 1740 map on the Atlas of Canada website.[23] It appears the Saugeen Ojibwa migrated to Saugeen Territory sometime between 1736 and 1788. They either migrated as two bands or expanded to two bands shortly after migration. Regardless, the Saugeen band's hunting territory was south of the Saugeen River to just north of Goderich and they fished on the Lake Huron side of the peninsula. The Nawash band hunted north of the Saugeen River and fished on the Georgian Bay side of the peninsula. There was also a small village of Ojibwa at Colpoy's Bay that had moved there from Coldwater in the late 1830s.

The Colonial Government of the day had a policy of assimilation called "civilization projects". These projects were modelled on the village set up by Peter Jones at the Credit. The Reverend Peter Jones was a Mississauga from the village near the mouth of the Credit River. He converted to Christianity and became a missionary in the Wesleyan Methodist Church. He worked with his own people to create a village much like the pioneer communities surrounding them. They had built a hospital, a schoolhouse attended by over forty children, a mechanic's shop, two sawmills, eight barns and over forty houses. They allocated nine hundred acres for farming and raised wheat, oats, peas, Indian corn, potatoes and other vegetables. Several Mississauga farmers cut hay and

---

22 "Enumeration of the Indian Tribes Connected with the Government of Canada; The Warriors and Armorial Bearings of Each Nation" dated 1736 at Missilimakinak printed in *Wisconsin Historical Collections*, Vol. XVII, 245-252.

23 http://atlas.gc.ca/site/english/maps/historical/aboriginalpeoples/circa1740 last accessed Aug. 15th, 2005.

had orchards.[24] This model was quite successful due to the understanding of Ojibwa culture by the Methodist missionaries. The Wesleyans had a policy of using converted Ojibwa leaders and using them as missionaries to their own people.

But the government did not work with the Wesleyan Methodists. They favoured the Church of England and so set up their own projects at Coldwater and the Narrows at present-day Orillia. Due to the authoritarian personalities of both the government officials and the Anglican missionaries their "civilization projects" did not work well.

Non-native interference began in 1829 with the arrival at Saugeen of Peter Jones to preach to the local residents. Due to his Ojibwa oratory skills and charismatic personality, he impressed the local Ojibwa including the main chief Kegedonce. After a trip to the Credit for a camp meeting and a tour of the Credit village, he converted to Christianity. His conversion led many other Saugeen Ojibwa to convert also. However, some remained traditionalists and vehemently opposed to Christianity. The Ojibwa at Nawash were not so receptive remaining a traditionalist stronghold as can be seen in the 1858 report in Appendix 1. In 1831 Kegedonce's lifeless body was found near Goderich and there was some dispute as to whether it was due to drowning or foul play.[25] Internal disputes and divisions due to outside influence had begun.

---

24 Smith, Donald B. *Sacred Feathers*, University of Toronto Press, Toronto: 1987, 145-146, 157.

25 See Kegedoons in Appendix 7.

CHAPTER 6

Treaty of 1836

In 1836 Sir Francis Bond Head was appointed Upper Canada's new lieutenant governor. The never-ending need for Ojibwa land to satisfy the requirements of the land speculators and their customers, the new arrivals from Europe, caused the government to look longingly at the Saugeen territory. It was the last large unceded Ojibwa territory in Southern Ontario. Bond Head had no faith in the government's policy of civilization projects. He thought they failed because the Ojibwa, being hunters and fishers, simply was not suited to a European farming lifestyle. He favoured a different policy, not unlike the American removal policy, but modelled on the Jesuit reductions in South America.[26]

Bond Head believed that the Ojibwa of Southern Ontario would be better off if they all congregated in one large territory. He also presumed this made for a better situation for the white settlers who were ever encroaching on Ojibwa lands. He chose Manitoulin Island as a site for his project because it was located a good distance from the white settlers and it was more conducive to the hunting and fishing lifestyle of the Ojibwa. He travelled from community to community throughout Upper Canada trying to convince the Ojibwa residents to give up their reserves and move north to Manitoulin. However, many in the southern part of the province had taken up the agrarian lifestyle and had settled into log or frame homes and had small working farms. They were not anxious to give up what had taken a lot

---

26 McMullen, Stephanie. *Disunity and Dispossession: Nawash Ojibwa and Potawatomi of the Saugeen Territory, 1836-1865.* (M.A. Thesis, University of Calgary, 1997) 30.

of hard work to accumulate. But others saw an advantage in one large "Indian Territory".

Wawanosh, the St. Clair chief endorsed a letter to the Christian Guardian, a Methodist periodical, proposing Upper Canada's Ojibwa population should settle together but not on Manitoulin Island. The letter supported a move to Saugeen Territory "because we can have roads from our settlements, the means of defence or flight in case of war at any future period ... we might be encouraged to be farmers." Furthermore, "our brethren at Sawgeeng pity us, as being so scattered, and are willing we should all come and settle with them in their country, on the most liberal terms."[27] However, few responded to either Bond Head's Manitoulin Island project or Wawanosh's letter. Most wanted to stay on their hard-earned farms and they had the backing of the Methodists and the Aborigines Protection Society in Britain.

Bond Head was still determined to acquire rich Saugeen lands for land-hungry settlers. At the annual present-giving ceremonies on Manitoulin Island in 1836, he called upon the Saugeen Ojibwa there to discuss the surrender of 1.5 million acres of their territory south of the Saugeen River to the northern boundary of the Huron Tract.

However, Bond Head wasn't aware of the Royal Proclamation of 1763 and the responsibilities it placed on the government. Instead of following its procedures, he cajoled and threatened the Saugeen representatives some of whom signed a surrender document. He told them that the Government could do nothing to prevent white settler encroachment on their lands and that if they did not surrender it to the government now they would lose everything. According to the Proclamation "if at any Time any of the said Indians should be inclined to dispose of the said Lands, the same shall be Purchased only for Us, in our Name, at some public Meeting or Assembly of the said Indians, to be held for the Purpose by the Governor or Commander in Chief of our Colony".[28] This treaty was illegally procured because it contravened both the Royal Proclamation of 1763 and Additional Instructions of 1794. Seven white men and only four Ojibwa signed it. Not only was there no general band

---

27 Ibid. 31, quoted from D.J. Bourgeois, "The Saugeen Indian Land Claim Re Treaty #45 ½, 1836" prepared for The Ontario Ministry of Natural Resources, 1985.

28 Ibid. "Excerpts from The Royal Proclamation of 1763" 109.

assembly called but also not all the Ojibwa that had a right to sign were there and those that were rejected the surrender. The Saugeen warriors refused to accept the capitulation of their leaders. Thomas Hurlburt, their missionary at the time, wrote later in the Christian Guardian of their discontent saying that for the last time in Upper Canada wampum belts were sent around encouraging others to "take up the hatchet".[29] Metiewabe, one of the Saugeen sub-chiefs signed the document because he was 'influenced by the fear of offending his Excellency." His did not have the authority to do so. The Saugeen Ojibwa had agreed beforehand that no person should be authorized to cede Saugeen territory without the consent obtained at a general council meeting and the agreement of the hereditary chiefs.[30]

There was considerable chagrin also expressed by the public through both the missionaries and the Aborigines' Committee of the Meeting for Sufferings. In the tract printed by the Meeting for Sufferings there is an extract from a letter published by Dr Edwin James, Indian Agent and Interpreter in which he writes, "Sir Francis Bond Head contrived to cheat them, or half cheat half bully them out of their lands at Saugeen, to remove them to settle on barren rocks, between whose interstices grew berries-Good enough feed for those Indians!"[31]

One of the signatories of Treaty # 45 ½, Joseph Stinson, General Superintendent of the Wesleyan Missions, gave this eyewitness account of Bond Head's meeting:

Sir Francis wished the Indians to surrender the whole of that territory to him; they declined; he endeavoured to persuade them, and even threatened them, by telling them that he could not keep the white people from taking possession of their land, that they (the Indians) had no right to it only as hunting grounds etc. They told him they could not live on the Munedoolin Island, that they would not go there, that they wanted land that they could call their own … The council of the Saugeen Indians separated. About an hour or two after, Sir Francis called them together again, renewed his proposals, persuasions and threats. The Indians refused. Sir Francis then proposed that if they would surrender to him

---

29 Smith, *Sacred Feathers*, 164.

30 Schmalz, *Ojibwa*, 136.

31 "The Report of the Aborigines' Committee of the Meeting for Sufferings", London: Harvey and Darton, 1840.

the territory adjoining the Canada Company's Huron tract, he would secure to them and their children the territory north of Owen Sound ... and build them houses on it from the sale of the territory ... To this purpose ... the poor Indians did readily accede with tears in their eyes.[32]

Unfortunately, the government accepted Bond Head's report at face value and approved his schemes. For a complete record of Bond Head's view of the transaction see appendix 2. The Saugeen Ojibwa never had their lands returned to them. The Saugeen band had lost their hunting and fishing territories and now the Saugeen (Bruce) peninsula containing 450,000 acres of mostly granite rock and bogs had to support three bands.

For the non-aboriginal protesters, the most contentious point of Treaty #45 ½ was that it contained no annuity clause. All previous land cession treaties contained some form of annuity provision so the Wesleyan Methodists joined the Aborigines' Protection Society in 1837 to protest. The government under attack from the humanitarian groups and needing native support because of the 1837 Rebellion in Upper Canada the government relented. Justice James McCauley, chair of an inquiry into Indian Affairs recommended some form of an annuity for Treaty #45 ½ in 1836. Samuel Jarvis, Superintendent General of Indian Affairs, agreed to an annuity of £500 in 1838. Finally, in 1840 an annuity was approved amounting to £2.10 for each member of the band to a maximum of 500 persons.[33]

---

32 Aborigines' Protection Society, *Tract Relative to the Aborigines* (London 1843), 16-20 reprinted in Schmalz, "Ojibwa", 136.

33 McMullen, *Disunity and Dispossession*, 33-34.

CHAPTER 7

Immigration of the 1830s and 1840s

During this period the reduced Saugeen territory saw an influx of newcomers. The government, trying to duplicate the Credit River Settlement's success at "Europeanizing the Indians", announced a new "civilization policy" where they would duplicate the Credit's community all over the province. The first two communities were to be established at Coldwater and the Narrows. Funding for the projects was secured in 1833. Lieutenant Governor Sir John Colborne appointed T.G Anderson as the Indian Agent. Anderson had been a trader on the Mississippi for years and was a British commander in the War of 1812. He understood the Ojibwa well but had trouble shaking his authoritarian character and his view of natives being minors. Although Colborne had told Mississauga Methodist missionary, Peter Jones, it didn't matter who educated them, in reality, he favoured the Church of England.[34] He then sent an Anglican minister and a white teacher to the projects with no native assistants. This only hurt the educational endeavour.

Many of the young men were not interested in trading the traditional way of life for a European farming one. During the planting season, they headed north to Georgian Bay to fish while the old men and young children were left to plant. They could not handle the laborious work so the farms that had been set up for them failed.

---

34 Smith, *Sacred Feathers*, 104.

Instead of offering encouragement and assistance to the two struggling Ojibwa settlements the surrounding white settlers only served to impede progress. In an 1835 article entitled "Anderson to Colborne" printed in the Christian Guardian Anderson was reported to have said the Ojibwa were "obliged frequently to submit to irritating and extremely unjust Treatment on the Part of the Neighbouring White Settlers".[35] All of these negative influences on the struggling young settlements as well as the internal strife between government and church denomination doomed them to failure. The two projects were abandoned in 1837 and the bands moved to other locations. One of these locations was Colpoy's Bay in Saugeen Territory where a small group of Ojibwa from Coldwater with some Mississauga from Lake Scugog settled.

The offer from the Saugeen Ojibwa to serve as a refuge for others still stood. Bond Head's removal project still had some life and a few of the educated and influential Ojibwa spoke for it at the Grand Council held July 4, 1845, at Saugeen. Forty-eight chiefs attended from Lakes St. Clair, Huron, Ontario, Simcoe, Rice and Mud. Chief John Jones from Nawash renewed the offer in his opening remarks. "Brothers! Some of you are living on small parcels of land, and others, on Islands. We now offer you any portion of the land which we own in this region; that we may, the rest of our days, smoke the pipe of friendship; live and die together; and see our children play, and be reared on one spot. We ask no money of you. We love you; and because we love you and feel for your children, we propose this."[36]

The Chief of the Saugeen band, David Sawyer, was a Mississauga from the Credit. He had taken advantage of the earlier offer when his whole reserve at the mouth of the Credit River had been ceded. However, most of the Mississauga of the Credit, upon seeing the rocky terrain of the Saugeen Peninsula, chose to take advantage of an offer of refuge from the Six Nations on the Grand River and moved there. Although the chiefs of the Grand Council were in favour of one "Indian Territory" their general population was not. Only a few individuals had bought into the idea and moved to Saugeen. By far the biggest influx was Potawatomi emigrating from the United States.

---

35 Schmalz, *Ojibwa*, 161.

36 Copway, George. *The Life, History, and Travels, of Kah-ge-ga-gah-bowh*, Albany: Weed and Parsons, 1847, 191.

Two reasons caused this great migration of Potawatomi into Upper Canada. The U.S. government was threatening them with removal from Michigan and Indiana to west of the Mississippi and the British Colonial government was about to enact a residency clause into their present giving policy. A Council was held August 20[th,] 1839 at Notawassippi, St. Joseph County, Michigan between the Potawatomi nation and the United States government. According to the Chicago Treaty, which ended the Black Hawk war, the Potawatomi were to "give up peaceable possession of the lands ceded to the government of the United States ... and remove west of the Mississippi River".[37] Chief Muckmote was adamant. "Father: We have held our consultation with the three nations, and what you said to us yesterday does not please us at all. You told us we must go west of the Mississippi. In our former councils we always said we would not go, and our minds have not changed yet. At the council at Niles the same question was put to us and we said we would not go. We say again, we will not go." After more dialogue, another Chief, Red Bird, concluded the council by saying "Father, you have heard our decision: we shall never go ... we will never meet in council again."[38]

Meanwhile, the American government relentlessly complained to the British about the handing out of presents to "American Indians" at Manitoulin and Walpole Islands. They felt that this only aggravated animosities felt toward the U.S. government and served to reinforce positive sentiments felt toward the British in Upper Canada. This was a practice that had gone on for decades and the presents represented recognition of services rendered as British allies through the War of 1812. The presents were being kept up to buy native support in case of more trouble with the United States. Many Potawatomi came from Michigan, Indiana and Wisconsin to receive these payments.

The British colonial government yielded to American complaints in the late 1830s and included a residency clause in their policy on present giving. The "visiting Indians" would no longer be eligible to receive government presents. They then renewed their longstanding invitation to their former allies to immigrate to Upper Canada, especially to the Saugeen Tract.[39]

---

37 "Indian Council" from the White Pigeon Republican, Aug. 28, 1839 reprinted in the *Historical Collections, Michigan Pioneer and Historical Society*, vol. X, 170.

38 Ibid. 172.

39 McMullen, *Disunity and Dispossession*, 37.

Thousands of new immigrants flooded into the country. One estimate of the number of Potawatomi arriving from Michigan, Indiana and Wisconsin between 1837 and 1849 was up to 3,000.[40] They crossed the border at Windsor and Sarnia in the south with many settling on Walpole Island. In one crossing alone three hundred Potawatomi refugees entered at Sarnia in July 1837. They were not totally welcomed at that reserve although a few stayed. They moved north with a few more staying at Kettle and Stoney Points, but the majority moved further north into the Saugeen tract. Many more Potawatomi arrived at Manitoulin Island in the North. However, Manitoulin only served as an entry point with the majority moving south into Saugeen territory looking for more fertile land.

The Nawash band welcomed the new immigrants. They saw them as a way to bolster their numbers to counteract the non-aboriginal population that was quickly growing near them, especially the community at Owen Sound. Of the Nawash band "313 of them lived at Nawash and Colpoy's Bay. Of these 118 were born in the United States or of American Born Parents. Twenty-eight more had one U.S.-born parent. 73 came from other settlements in Upper Canada, and 28 more had at least one parent from another Upper Canadian village. Only 52 people were actually born in the Saugeen Territory of Saugeen parents.[41] The Saugeen band was not so accommodating. After a few initial immigrants arrived they refused to accommodate any more. The Bagot Commission reported that in1845 "their present number is 197, including about a score of Pottawatomies."[42] However, later the Saugeen band took a softer line with the newcomers and by 1907 there were as many Potawatomi residents as Ojibwa.[43] Needless to say, all this immigration had serious consequences for Saugeen. Before 1836 the territory was over 2.5 million acres and supported 327 people. By 1850 the reduced territory of 450,000 acres had to support three bands totalling more than twice the original population.

---

40 Rogers and Smith, *Aboriginal Ontario*, 123.

41 NAC, RG 31, 1851 census, Derby Township (Indian Territory), C-11723 cited in McMullen, *Disunity and Dispossession*, fn 2, 54.

42 "Report of the Affairs of the Indians in Canada", *Journal of the Legislative Assembly of the Province of Canada*, Vol. 4, Appendix EEE, 43.

43 McMullen, *Disunity and Dispossession*, fn 36, 39.

CHAPTER 8

Surrenders of the 1850s

"The whole white race is a monster who is always hungry and what he eats is land."—Chiksika, Shawnee. Over the two decades that followed the 1836 treaty, which ceded the southern part of Saugeen territory began to fill with white settlers. They cleared the land for farms and small communities had begun to spring up. More and more immigrants were arriving from Europe and they were looking for land to farm. The colonial government began to look to the Saugeen peninsula to satisfy this need. The bands at Saugeen, Nawash and Colpoy's Bay resisted.

Since the 1840s the white settlers had called upon the government to build a road between their settlements of Owen Sound and Southampton. The government finally responded in 1851 but rather than build the road on existing farmland they wanted the Ojibwa to surrender a half-mile wide strip of land from their reserve to accommodate the road. Some in the Nawash and Saugeen communities saw an advantage in a road, as it would also connect their two communities making travel for them much easier as well. However, the three bands were wary of treaty negotiations having seen the government fail to uphold treaty responsibilities so often in the past. The agent, T.G. Anderson persisted and eventually convinced them to sign the treaty surrendering the 4800 acres needed for the road allowance. Although this treaty is mentioned in Treaties 72 and 82 it is not included in the three-volume set, Indian Treaties and Surrenders.

The sea of non-aboriginals arriving from Europe and the land speculators hungry for even more profits exerted pressure on the colonial government for more agricultural land. They looked enviously at the peninsula. The land in the southern part was fertile and suitable for agricultural use. At a General Council meeting at Saugeen on October 30, 1852, the Saugeen, Nawash and Colpoy's Bay bands decided to meet together to discuss common business, including … treaty negotiations, before any of the bands made decisions.[44] The Indian Department ignored the bands' wishes. The Central Superintendent of the Indian Department, T.G. Anderson, approached the Saugeen bands in August of 1854 about a surrender of the whole Saugeen Peninsula. The Saugeen bands were adamantly against any new surrender. They were still waiting for some movement on the road to be built along the "half-mile strip" given up in 1851. They also were expecting new arrivals from other native communities because of the generous offer to move there made at a recent General Council at Saugeen, 29 August 1853. They felt the need to honour their word to their fellow countrymen.

Anderson persisted using the old strategy of "divide and conquer". He told them that many were getting no benefit from the land but all would profit from it if they surrendered it. He knew that only 343 Saugeen and Nawash Ojibwa were entitled to the £1250 annuity from the 1836 surrender but their population had greatly increased. At first, the bands remained firm, but after deliberating for an hour amongst themselves they capitulated. However, they proposed limits on the plans for four reserves totalling 34,000 acres shown on Anderson's map. Of the 190,000 acres south of Colpoy's Bay and the Fishing Islands "130,000 acres is included within the two parcels desired to be retained by the Indians, including all the coast, both of Georgian Bay and Lake Huron".[45]

Anderson resorted to threats, an old ploy used in acquiring the 1836 surrender. He told them "After talking all day yesterday and nearly all last night, on the subject of your reserve, you have concluded not to cede your land to the Government …You complain that the whites not only cut and take your timber from your land, but that they are commencing to settle upon it, and you cannot prevent them, and I certainly do not think that the Government will take the trouble to help you … The Government has the power to act as it pleases with your reserve … I will

44 McMullen, *Disunity and Dispossession*, 61.

45 . "Sub-enclosure 3, to Enclosure in No. 1", *Indian Department (Canada), Return to an Address of the Honourable The House of Commons*, 28th April 1856, 13. See Appendix 3 for the complete sub-enclosure.

recommend that the whole, excepting the parts marked on the map in red and blue [Government's layout of land to be reserved] be surveyed and sold for the good of yourselves and your children … whereas, if it is not sold, the trees and land will be taken from you by your white neighbours and your children will be left without resource." Anderson could not see any validity in the objections to the surrender: "in two days council they did not advance one good argument why the reserve should not be sold beyond, 'We don't want to sell our land,' 'We want to keep it for our children,' 'We expect Indians to come here to settle,' &c., &c.,"[46] However, the bands remained united in their opposition.

The General Superintendent of Indian Affairs, Lawrence Oliphant, got involved. He realized that jealousies between the bands at Saugeen and Nawash were present. They were caused by the feelings held by the Saugeen band that "they were first established in this part of the peninsula, and therefore consider that they occupy the most prominent position in the tribe, and are entitled to a larger share in its councils".[47] Oliphant perceived that this had caused Anderson problems at the August 2nd council at Owen Sound. He also thought there was an advantage in having the young men and warriors of Saugeen present at this council. They were absent from the Owen Sound council. The other chiefs arrived on the afternoon of October 13th, 1854 and not wishing to allow them to deliberate amongst themselves Oliphant called a council for 7 o'clock that evening.

At first, under the influence of Saugeen principal chief Alexander Madwayosh, the bands were not receptive to surrender. Oliphant echoed Anderson's threats. After compelling them to complain about white encroachments on their lands he said: "I represented the extreme difficulty, if not impossibility, of preventing such unauthorized intrusion." If they sold their lands the proceeds would pay for farm improvements and schools. He then made four more promises. He promised them the surrendered land would be surveyed and sold at auction, that the annuities arising would be paid in money and not in goods, that they would receive titles to farm lots, granted by the government, on their

---

46 Ibid. "Sub-enclosure 2, to Enclosure in No. 1" 12-13.

47 Ibid. 4.

reserved lands, and those chiefs who signed the treaty would be rewarded by your Excellency with medals. [48]

He retired from the council for an hour to let the Chiefs have a private debate and when he returned he found that Chief Madwayosh had been completely out-voted. After some conciliations made on both sides regarding the lands to be reserved for them, Treaty 72 was signed and the council adjourned at 1 o'clock A.M. (See Sketch in Appendix 4 for locations of reserves).

According to Oliphant's official report "Immediately on my arrival at Saugeen, I despatched messengers for the chiefs of the Saugeen band, who were absent at their fishing grounds, as well as those of the Owen Sound and Colpoy's Bay bands"[49] Conrad Van Dusen, the Methodist missionary at Nawash, had quite a different account. He reports that "When Mr Oliphant ... came ... to treat with the Indians for the surrender of their peninsula, he passed by the band at Nawash without even letting them know of his arrival or the object of his visit". Van Dusen also challenged Oliphant's report that all the chiefs of the different bands attended the council. He claims that not one chief from Colpoy's Bay attended and that the chiefs from Nawash did not reach Saugeen until the next day just in time to sign the treaty, but missed out on the deliberations. John Beaty was the only member of the Colpoy's Bay band that attended only because he happened to be there. He was asked to represent Colpoy's Bay, which he agreed to do and he signed the treaty although he was never a chief. Because the Royal Proclamation of 1763 was ignored again, this treaty appears to also be invalid as there was no band membership vote held for Nawash or Colpoy's Bay nor was there an opportunity for the chiefs of all three bands to deliberate the matter[50].

Both Anderson and Oliphant told the Saugeen Ojibwa the government could do nothing about the squatters on their land. But, upon arriving at Owen Sound the day after the treaty was signed, Oliphant issued a notice warning squatters from trespassing on lands

---

48 Ibid.

49 Ibid.

50 Van Dusen, Conrad. *The Indian Chief*, (1867: 51-60) reprinted as Appendix 1 in Elizabeth Graham, *Medicine Man to Missionary*, Toronto: Peter Martin Associates, 1975, 93-97.

recently surrendered to the Crown and also wrote to the sheriff asking him for his assistance in this matter.[51]

Oliphant predicted in his report to Lord Elgin that because of the close proximity of two of the reserves to established white communities at Southampton and Owen Sound that further surrenders would be necessary. He was correct. Just over two years later the village of Owen Sound incorporated as a town. The town wanted to expand and they coveted the land across the Potawatomi River, the Nawash reserve. Colonial legislators supported the idea of a surrender so ordered the Indian Agent, W.R. Bartlett to obtain one. Again the government put intense pressure on the Nawash band using the same tactics of threats sweetened with promises but to no avail.

The village at Nawash had undergone great changes over a fifteen-year period. Several permanent houses had been build as well as barns. Fields had been cultivated and docks had been built and public buildings constructed. They were resolute to keep their hard-earned assets. However, the attitudes of the government and the general population toward the aboriginals had changed. "Civilization projects" had fallen out of favour. The idea of moving the Nawash band to the Cape Croker reserve seemed a good solution to the whites but not to the band members. They knew that although they were promised farm lots and houses for individuals the land there was not suitable enough either for agriculture or hunting.

The government knew there were internal divisions and animosities among the band leadership. The Ojibwa were most resolute not to surrender any more land. The Potawatomi had been easier to work with in the past because they feared deportation to the U.S. if they angered the government. The Indian Department tried their "divide and conquer" strategy working with the Potawatomi faction of the band only, but still to no avail. After months of cajoling, finagling and threats they were still no closer to a surrender treaty.

After further threats the Indian Department finally got a few to relent and agree to surrender the Nawash reserve. They arranged to have them travel to Toronto in February 1857 for the official signing of the treaty. Here is another illegal treaty due to another violation of the

---

51 Ibid. See Sub-enclosure 5 and Sub-enclosure 6.

Proclamation of 1763 as no public meeting was held for the purpose of debate.

Upon hearing about the surrender the Ojibwa at Nawash were dismayed. The Potawatomi left almost immediately for the Cape. The Ojibwa, on the other hand, repudiated the treaty and refused to leave their lands at Nawash. Despite this refusal, the Nawash lands went up for auction in September 1857. The Ojibwa attended the auction and even bid on their own land, but the government refused to recognise their bids. Because they were not citizens of Upper Canada they did not have the right to own private property so they were forced to relocate.

The government continued to put pressure on for more land, especially between 1859 and 1861. Finally, the Colpoy's Bay band surrendered their 6,000-acre reserve on August 16, 1861. Many of them moved to Christian Island and Rama but some moved with relatives at Cape Croker. This left only two Ojibwa communities in Saugeen Territory, the Ojibwa of Saugeen and the Ojibwa of Nawash holding joint ownership of the islands of Lake Huron and Georgian Bay. In 1885 the two bands surrendered two groups of islands. Known as the Saugeen Fishing Islands and Cape Hurd Islands they represented the final assault on Saugeen Territory and the turbulent surrender period ended. From this point forward the government would deal with Saugeen and Nawash as separate entities.

CHAPTER 9

Paternalism 1860-1900

The assimilation policy in Canada would be taken up in earnest when the responsibility for Indian affairs was transferred to the government of Upper Canada in 1860. This policy remained official government policy for over one hundred years. The cornerstone of this process would be the residential school. These would come under the jurisdiction of the federal government, but the responsibility of day-to-day operations would lay with the Church. Numerous manual labour schools were founded between 1842 and 1878.[52]

The complicity of the Church with the policy of total cultural replacement can be seen in a letter from the Rev. Alexander Sutherland, general secretary of the Methodist Church of Canada, Missionary Department, to Laurence Vankoughnet, deputy superintendent general of Indian affairs: "Experience convinces us that the only way in which the Indian of the country can be permanently elevated and thoroughly civilized is by removing the children from the surroundings of Indian home life, and keeping them separated long enough to form those habits of order, industry, and systematic effort, which they will never learn at home".[53]

Edward Francis Wilson established the Shingwauk residential school for boys at Sault Ste. Marie, Ontario, in 1873. Wilson was an Anglican missionary sent to Canada by the English Church Missionary Society. He was the school's first principal and remained in that post until 1893. All residential schools had the aim of providing the environment for as total a cultural replacement as possible, and Shingwauk was no exception.

---

52 Schmalz, *The Ojibwa of Southern Ontario*, 181-184.

53 Ibid. 181.

Language was seen as a major key in the cultural replacement program. First Nations languages were not allowed to be spoken during school, chores or play. In order to enforce the ban, a scheme was devised by Wilson in which children were rewarded for checking up on each other. When this failed, corporal punishment was meted out during the punishment period at seven in the evening. This policy against the children speaking their own language remained in effect until 1971.

Prohibition against all other forms of culture was also included in the residential schools' rules. At play, the children were not allowed to play First Nations games but were made to play European games such as marbles, cricket and soccer. First Nations forms of music were also forbidden. Shingwauk, like other residential schools, formed a marching band where the boys learned to play European marches and hymns. Other European cultural forms were forced upon the children, such as the celebration of western holidays like Christmas, Easter and Dominion Day. Of course, participation in any First Nations feasts or religious ceremonies was strictly forbidden. These assimilationist policies continued well into the twentieth century.[54]

The single most influential object used by the government of Canada to control the lives of First Nations people was the Indian Act of 1876. Its control was dictatorial and its influence suffocating. "As a deputy minister of the Indian Affairs Branch noted: 'The Indian Act is a Land Act. It is a Municipal Act, an Education Act and a Societies Act. It is primarily social legislation, but has a very broad scope; there are provisions about liquor, agriculture and mining as well as Indian lands, band membership and so forth. It has elements that are embodied in perhaps two dozen different acts of any of the provinces and overrides some federal legislation in some respects . . . It has the force of the Criminal Code and the impact of a constitution on those people and communities that come within its purview.'"[55]

---

54 For an excellent exposé on E.F. Wilson and his days as principal of the Shingwauk residential school see David A. Nock, *A Victorian Missionary and Canadian Indian Policy*, (Waterloo: Wilfred Laurier University. 1988), 67-100.

55 Schmalz, *Ojibway*, 196 quoting Franz M. Koennecke, "Wasoksing: The History of Parry Island, an Anishnabwe Community in the Georgian Bay, 1850-1920.", MA Thesis, University of Waterloo, 1984, 263.

One amendment to the Act in 1884 "imposed two to six month's imprisonment on anyone participating in certain Indian religious acts".[56] It was amended again in 1889 to allow "greater federal government control over Indian education, morality, local government and land. For example, the Ojibwa's most valued possession, their land, could be taken without their consent for leasing to non-Indians".[57]

Enfranchisement was the most discriminatory section. It allowed a First Nations man to gain all the rights and privileges of Canadians, including citizenship and the right to vote and hold office, if he were to allow the registrar to remove his name from the Indian Register. He lost his birthright, including treaty rights and band rights, which also included the right to live and hold land on his reserve. In effect, he became a white man in everything but colour. This section was forced on First Nations women when they married a non-First Nations man. It was also amended in 1880 to force enfranchisement on First Nations people who graduated from university, gained a profession or became ordained. The amendment "declared that any Indian with a university degree would ipso facto be enfranchised and therefore no longer be an Indian under the act".[58] Although enfranchisement was finally repealed in 1984 some sub-sections were repealed earlier.[59]

The practice of patronage appointments was the mechanism used to enforce the Indian Act. Bureaucrats called Indian Agents were appointed to serve on reserves in order to enforce the act locally on First Nations people and their assets.[60]

Indian Agents had such absolute power over the life of First Nations communities that the people viewed the government as a dictatorship. The Church was also viewed as a part of that dictatorship because, to a certain extent, the local minister or priest shared in this power imposed on them. Basil Johnston of Cape Croker, poignantly describes his 1939

---

56 Schmalz, Ojibwa, 205.

57 Ibid. 207.

58 Ibid. 198.

59 For a good overview of the 1857 Enfranchisement Act see Rogers and Smith, eds., Aboriginal Ontario, 199-201 and for the 1885 Franchisement Act, 235-239.

60 Schmalz, *The Ojibwa of Southern Ontario*, 212.

childhood experience of being sent to the residential school in Spanish, Ontario:

> The reason for and the mode of my own committal were typical. My parents had separated, and, following the break-up, Mother, my four sisters and I lived with my grandmother for a while.
>
> But unknown to either my mother or my grandmother, the Indian agent and the priest has conferred – with nothing but our welfare in mind, of course – and decided that not even the combined efforts of Grandmother and Mother were enough to look after five children and that they ought to be relieved of two of their burdens . . .
>
> On the fateful day, Grandmother and Mother wept as they scrubbed and polished and clothed me in the finest second-hand clothing that they had been able to scrounge at the bazaar . . .
>
> Mr. F. Tuffnel did not come in as invited; instead he stood at the doorway, glowering through his rimless glasses and pursing his mouth as if afraid to open it lest he be contaminated.
>
> Mr. Tuffnel unstitched his lips after looking at me and rasped, 'Well! Where's the other one?'
>
> 'She's sick,' Mother replied in her best English. 'Got poison ivy, her . . . in bed.' . . .
>
> The agent flinched perhaps not wanting to catch poison ivy. 'Well, gotta take two at least,' he said . . . 'How about her?' he rasped, pointing at . . . my four year old sister.

Mother and Grandmother were both appalled. 'No! She's too young,' they wailed. 'She can't go to school yet, she's only four. No!'

But the agent knew how to handle Indians, especially Indian women. 'Well, if you don't want her to go, we'll take the whole family. Now! Get her ready. Hurry up!'

Mother and Grandmother whimpered as they washed and clothed my sister.[61]

Indeed, the Indian agent had sweeping powers, powers far greater than any chief had under traditional government. Nothing came into the community or left the community without his approval. No band resolution was valid unless he passed them onto the Department of Indian Affairs for their approval. In fact, no band council meeting had any power unless he was present. Their duties involved corresponding with the federal government on every circumstance. He was the sole purchasing agent for the community, buying all the cattle, seed and farm implements. He was also the sole selling agent, responsible for selling the farm produce. He managed the community's bank accounts. He tendered and oversaw all building construction. He also acted as judge in civil disputes and was the inspector of education in the community.[62] Unfortunately, because of the system of patronage appointments, very rarely were Indian agents of the quality essential to undertake such responsibilities. Consequently, it was the First Nations and their communities that suffered.

I do not intend to paint a picture of total corruption and abuse. There were some good Indian agents. There were also many good missionaries, ministers and priests. Many of these spoke out against the oppressive domination of the prevalent society, but they were visionaries far ahead of their time and notably in the minority.

One such figure was Froome Talfourd. He took over the visiting superintendency at St. Clair in 1858. Upon doing so, he found that

---

61 Basil H. Johnston, *Indian School Days* (Toronto: Key Porter Books, 1988), 19-20.

62 Schmalz, *Ojibway*, 208.

there had been numerous complaints about missing monies from land transactions and late payments from such large corporations as the Grand Western Railway Company. He investigated and found the discrepancies in the Land Account Books indicated that embezzlement was involved. He reported this to Lord Bury, the superintendent general of Indian affairs.[63]

This was one of many incidents in which Talfourd stood up on the side of his First Nations charge. So fair, honest and upright was he in his dealings with the St. Clair First Nation that he quickly gained a highly regarded reputation among them, so much so, in fact, that the community instituted a feast in his honour that was still being celebrated one hundred years later. Nicholas Plain writes in his 1951 short history, "Among the Indians, he was known as 'The Englishman who keeps his word.' . . . The Indians of the Sarnia Reserve tendered him a banquet on his birthday, November 4th . . . The Talfourd Feast was one event in the year that no Indian missed. Even the aged and sick had steaming plates of food delivered to their homes."[64] The Talfourd Feast was still being celebrated as I was growing up during the 1950s.

During the months of March through June 1891, a series of four articles appeared in The Canadian Indian under the pseudonym of "Fair Play".[65] The articles advocated cultural synthesis rather than cultural replacement (forced assimilation). Cultural synthesis is defined as encouraging "the synthesis of two cultures, that retains the elements of both, and that encourages the voluntary borrowing and adaptation by the weaker cultural system . . . the cultural components from different societies will be combined in ways that make sense to the borrowing society".[66]

The articles also advocated a high degree of political autonomy. "He suggests it would constitute no harm or menace to Canada if the Indians

---

63 Ibid. 169-170.

64 Nicholas Plain (Osarskedawa), *The History of Chippewas of Sarnia and the History of Sarnia Reserve* (Sarnia, ON: Privately Printed, 1951), 30.

65 Nock argues that the author of the "Fair Play" articles was E.F. Wilson, despite the fact that the thrust of the articles went against the grain of the policies of the Shingwauk residential school, an institution founded and run for the first twenty years by him. See David A. Nock, *A Victorian Missionary*, 135-150.

66 Ibid. 1-2.

of Ontario 'were permitted to have their own centre of Government –
their own Ottawa, so to speak; their own Lieutenant-Governor, and their
own Parliament'".[67] During the latter half of the 19th-century paternalism
in its many forms reached its zenith much to the detriment of the First
Nations of Canada.

---

67 Ibid. 136 quoting Fair Play, "The Future of Our Indians," Paper No. 3, *The
Canadian Indian* 1, no. 9 (June 1891), 254.

CHAPTER 10

Modern Times

After World War II both the government and the public at large began to question Canada's Indian Policy. A joint committee of House Representatives and the Senate was formed to study the matter. As a result, the Indian Act of 1876 underwent extensive revision. First Nations people regained the right to attend traditional religious ceremonies, to drink alcohol in public places such as bars and taverns, and compulsory enfranchisement ended (except in the case of native women marring non-native men). The revised Act also gave individual band councils more authority.[68] Assimilation was still the government's official policy but it would now be allowed to happen gradually and would not be forced upon First Nations.

The assimilation policy culminated with Pierre Elliott Trudeau's Liberal Government and its 1969 White Paper. This was the last official blueprint for cultural replacement and assimilation. It proposed to terminate all special rights and separate recognition of First Nations including the Indian Act, reserves and treaties. In return, First Nations people would receive the same legal rights and recognition as other Canadians.[69]

First Nations vehemently opposed the policy. For example, Chief Fred Plain, president of the Union of Ontario Indians at the time, countered the policy by presenting "a brief to Ottawa which would give twelve seats in the House of Commons to Indian representatives . . .

---

68 Rogers and Smith, *Aboriginal Ontario*, 396.

69 Ibid. n18, 9.

He pointed out that New Zealand already had such a plan in effect for its Maori population".[70] This plan was not adopted, but because of the massive opposition to the White Paper, it was formally withdrawn in 1971.

In 1970, Jeannette (Corbière) Lavell of Manitoulin Island registered an injunction prohibiting the registrar from removing her name from the Indian Register because she married a non-First Nations person. She used the Bill of Rights clause against sexual discrimination and won in the lower courts. However, she lost in the Supreme Court. The Indian Act took precedence over the Bill of Rights. On the other hand, Sandra Lovelace of the Tobique Reserve in New Brunswick took her similar case to the United Nations. In 1981 Canada was found in violation of an international covenant on human rights. As a result, the Indian Act was rewritten to remove sexual discrimination and married First Nations women and their children were allowed to regain lost status.[71]

Land claims have proliferated the 20th century. In 1994 the Ojibwa of Saugeen and Nawash filed a joint statement of claim against Ontario and Canada. The MEDIA RELEASE 14 JUNE 1994 read in part:

"Nawash & Saugeen First Nations - On May 27th, 1994, the Saugeen and Nawash Ojibway filed a statement of claim against Ontario and Canada for a breach of their fiduciary obligations to the First Nations in the negotiations and signing of the Treaty of 1854. The Saugeen and Nawash Ojibway are also asserting ownership of road allowances currently vested in nine municipal defendants in Grey and Bruce Counties. Together the Saugeen and Nawash Ojibway signed the 1836 Treaty, which resulted in the loss of one and a half million acres of their traditional territory just south of what is now the Bruce Peninsula. In return for all that land, the First Nations got a promise that Canada would protect their fishery as well as their new home, the Bruce Peninsula. In 1854, they signed another treaty which resulted in the loss of the Peninsula itself (some 500,000 acres) It is in the signing of the 1854 Treaty that the Saugeen and Nawash Ojibway allege Canada breached its fiduciary, or trust-like, obligation with the First Nations,"

---

70 Schmalz, *Ojibwa*, 251.

71 Schmalz, *Ojibwa*. 256-257.

The Saugeen and Nawash First Nations laid claim to the lakebed of Lake Huron and Georgian Bay as well in 2004. This media release reads in part,

Bruce Peninsula, Ontario—On December 23, 2003, The Chippewas of Nawash Unceded First Nation and the Chippewas of Saugeen First Nation filed an extensive claim with the Ontario Superior Court asserting aboriginal title to their traditional territories under the waters of Lake Huron and Georgian Bay. The claim is against Canada as a descendant of the "Crown" that negotiated treaties with First Nations in Ontario and against Ontario, which has assumed possession of lands named in the claim. Although lands under water were clearly the subjects of other Treaties (notably in the US), they were not mentioned in any of the Treaties the Crown signed with the First Nations in the Saugeen Ojibway Nations Territories (the traditional territories of the Chippewas of Nawash and Saugeen). The two First Nations are claiming aboriginal title to the lands under the water covering an area of Lake Huron and Georgian Bay from south of Goderich, west to the international border and north to the mid-point between the tip of the Bruce Peninsula and Manitoulin Island; then east to the mid-point of Georgian Bay and south to the southern-most point of Nottawasaga Bay.[72]

The bands' Legal researcher said, "The breach is not in that the Crown failed to do what it said it would do in the Treaty of 1854. It is the Treaty itself. What we're saying by this action is that by getting us to sign the treaty of 1854, the Crown did not live up to the standards of high behaviour it set for itself in previous legislation. We're not saying the treaty is invalid, but we are saying the situation the Treaty left us in deserves remedy." Land being claimed in the suits amount to 55,000 acres. Compensation being claimed for loss of use and the present value of lands not recoverable because private parties now own them is $80 billion. A further $10 billion in compensation is being asked for as punitive damages. A court date is expected to be set for 2018.

72 Press releases can be seen at http://www.turtleisland.org/discussion/viewtopic. php?p=2116 last accessed August 26,2005.

Culture

CHAPTER 11

Ojibwa Characteristics

From first contact with the Europeans, the Ojibwa were looked upon as "hospitable, proud, redoubtable to their enemies" and "very industrious ... the tribe had many brave warriors. These were feared and respected by all the other tribes around the Great Lakes. Warriors of this tribe were among the first in historic times to defeat the Iroquois."[73] The first to make contact with the Ojibwa was Samuel de Champlain. He called them Cheveux-Relevés or the 'high hairs'. After "having visited seven or eight of their villages [Petun], the explorers pushed forward still further west, when they came to the settlement of an interesting tribe, which they named 'Cheveux-Relevés' or the 'lofty haired', an appellation suggested by the mode of dressing their hair."[74] They are described as follows, "These are savages that wear nothing about the loins, and go stark naked, except in the winter, when they clothe themselves in robes of skins, which they leave off when they quit their houses for the fields. They are great hunters, fishermen, and travellers, till the soil, and plant Indian corn. They dry bluets [blueberries] and raspberries, in which they carry on an extensive traffic with other tribes, taking in exchange skins, beads, nets, and other articles. Some of these people pierce their nose, and attach beads to it. They tattoo their bodies, applying black and other colours.

---

73 Kinietz, *Indians*, 320-21.

74 Voyages of Samuel de Champlain 1537-1635, Vol. 1, trans. Charles Pomeroy Otis PhD. The Prince Society, Boston: 1880, 139.

They wear their hair very straight, and grease it, painting it red, as they do also the face."[75]

The Ojibwa arrived in Saugeen Territory shortly after the Iroquois War. During the Traditional Period ca 1700-1836 they lived the traditional semi-nomadic life. The main village was at the mouth of the Saugeen River where they would spend the summer and fall collectively hunting, fishing and gathering. During this time they would also make trips to Fort Pontchartrain [Detroit] to trade pelts for European goods. After the fall gatherings [Powwows], usually held at Boweeting most would disperse into their hunting territory in smaller groups to spend the winter hunting and trapping. In the months of February and March, they would move to their sugar camps to make maple sugar products, which they used for cooking and for trade. They then moved to their fishing camps for the spring fish runs and after this, they all returned to congregate at the main village for the summer and fall.

It is said by some modern historians that the First Nations were great stewards of the land and were among the earth's first conservationists. These kinds of statements are the result of a lack of understanding of First Nation philosophy. The Ojibwa did not see themselves as somehow separate from nature with a need to "look after it". This is a modern western concept that flows out of their earlier Biblical based idea that they were to "have dominion and subdue" the earth and its resources. Instead, the Ojibwa saw themselves as being a part of nature. Indeed, they even saw themselves as being the weakest part needing both the Creator's help through the muneedoos and the help of the game itself. They believed that animals had the ability to choose whether to give their lives for the sustenance of the people, which they often did according to the wishes of the Creator. Hence, the practice of giving a tobacco offering when game was taken or for the use of resources such as trees for shelter or utensils.

Ojibwa philosophy was Platonic in nature. They thought that the physical world they lived in was only an image of the real world. The link between the two lay in dreams. So this made dreams and their interpretations extremely important and they lived their daily lives accordingly.

---

75 Ibid. 303.

CHAPTER 12

Language[76]

There were three linguistic groups living in the Great Lakes Basin or interacting with the Ojibwa nation. They were Siouan, Iroquoian and Algonquian speaking peoples. Some examples of nations speaking a Sioux language were Dakota, Lakota, Nakota, and Otchente Chakowin. The Winnebago or Puants were also of the Siouan linguistic group as were the Assiniboin. The nations speaking Iroquoian were the Huron, the Tobacco Nation (Tionontati) the Neutral Nation, the Erie and the St. Lawrence Iroquois. Members of the Five Nation Confederacy also spoke Iroquoian languages. These were the Mohawk, Onondaga, Oneida, Cayuga and Seneca nations.

The largest linguistic group in the area was by far the Algonquian group. Speakers of this language stock included the Cree, Menominee, Sauk, Fox, Kickapoo, Miami, Illinois, Shawnee, and Delaware, as well as the members of the Three Fires Confederacy, the Ojibwa, Ottawa and Potawatomi. By the time the Ojibwa moved into Saugeen Territory the Erie, St. Lawrence, and Neutral Iroquois had disappeared and the remnants of the Huron and Tionontati had merged to become the Wyandotte. One can see by this list the diversity of languages spoken in the Great Lakes area.

The Ojibwa language was so close to the Ottawa language that the two had no trouble understanding one another. In fact, Ottawa is really an Ojibwa dialect that had deviated farthest but still belongs to the

---

76 Rhodes, Richard. *Eastern Ojibwa-Chippewa-Ottawa Dictionary*, Mouton de Gruyter, New York, 1993 pp x, xi, xxiv, xxv.

Southern Ojibwa group of dialects. "The Ottawa dialect is also known as Chippewa or Ojibwa in Michigan and the adjacent region of Southern Ontario. This comes from the fact that many speakers of Ottawa there are descendants of Chippewas who, during the 1800's, moved into areas where Ottawa was the dialect spoken. Sometimes Ottawa speakers will say that the language they speak is a mixture of Ottawa and Chippewa ... which reflects a linguistic reality arising from the historical fact."

The southern group also includes Eastern Ojibwa. Eastern Ojibwa is the dialect spoken on the eastern shore of Georgian Bay east to the Algonquin dialect, which for example is spoken on the Golden Lake and Maniwaki reserves.

There are two other distinct groups of Ojibwa dialects. There is a northern group comprising of Severn Ojibwa in Northern Ontario (know locally as Cree) and the Algonquin group mentioned above, which is spoken in South-western Quebec. The dialect spoken by the Saugeen Ojibwa like other Ojibwa dialects were no doubt impacted by the interjection of Potawatomi words brought by the Potawatomi who settled among them in the 1800's.

There are a large number of variations heard among Ojibwa speakers. They range from differences in pronunciation to varying forms of the same words to entirely different words and even different constructions are found. Some variations are personal in nature and some are a result of different ethnic or geographic roots. For example, all Ottawa and Chippewa speakers pronounce b, d, g, etc. at the end of words as if they were p, t, k, and etc. respectively. So they pronounce naasaab (the same) as though it were naasaap, and kaad (leg) as laat. Speakers of Eastern Ojibwa never do this. Every community has variations within it, as do individual families. For example, some speakers pronounce the word meaning winter as poon, or boon or bboon.

A speaker's choice of some words can distinguish the dialect he or she is speaking very clearly. For example, Ottawa and Chippewa speakers call the sugar maple sinaamizh, but Eastern Ojibwa speakers call the sugar maple ninaatig. Sometimes the choice of the word occurs with a dialect. For example, some Ottawa and Chippewa speakers will call a tool aabjichgan while others call it nokaazwin. Likewise, most Eastern Ojibwa speakers call a table wiisniwaagan but some call it doopwin.

There are many English words borrowed by the Ojibwa speaker. Generally speaking the further north the community the less borrowing is seen. U.S. Ottawa or Chippewa speakers will call electricity 'power' while Ontario speakers borrow the word 'hydro'. Some borrowed words that contain r or l undergo an adjustment toward Ojibwa phonology. For example, Mary or Marie becomes Maanii and Charlie becomes Chaalii. This applies to the letter v as well. My name is David as is my son's. At Aamjiwnaang we are called Chi-Dabid (Big David) and Dabidiins (Little David) respectively. Time is told in English but the hour is expressed as 'clock' not 'o'clock'. Aanii-sh e-piichi-yaag? Two Clock. What time is it? Two o'clock.

CHAPTER 13

Religion

The Ojibwa world was both a corporeal and a spiritual world at once. Their daily lives were inspired by the interaction of spiritual beings that affected the everyday activities of their physical world. A spirit being commonly called a manitou is more properly called a muneedoo, although the meaning of the word is not limited to spirit. It can also refer to the essence, characteristic or power of a thing such as a plant or a ceremony. Needless to say, this caused much confusion for the early Christian missionaries. Of these spiritual beings, there was one overall and creator of all. This spirit being was known as Kitchi-Muneedoo or the Great Mystery.

Kitchi-Muneedoo was transcendental, unknowable and therefore shrouded in mystery. However, it was believed that he was the creator of all things including the other muneedoos. In the creation story, Kitchi-Muneedoo created the heavenly expanse, in which he placed the sun and moon and a myriad of stars. He created the earth and all that is in it, the rivers and lakes, plants and trees, birds, fish and animals all according to his vision. He also created the Ahnishenahbek or the real people. He also created the spiritual realm and all the muneedoos according to the purpose of his vision. One of these kinds of muneedoos were personal spirit beings and their purpose was to act as a guide and helper in the Ahnishenahbi's life as well an intercessor between the person and Kitchi-Muneedoo.

This creation story demonstrates a belief in God and an understanding of the origin of things. It also served as an example for the Ahnishenahbek to follow and so the tradition of seeking their personal muneedoos through a vision or dream was developed. In this tradition, a young person of puberty or adolescent age would prepare himself for his vision quest by purifying himself in the sweat lodge ceremony. When this was completed he would seek out a place to meditate in the wilds preferably a high place where the wind was constant. There he would fast and meditate until his vision came. This vision would always contain a central figure represented by an animal, bird, reptile or some other creature and this would be his personal muneedoo. This muneedoo would have the characteristics of the corporeal representation and would use them in his interaction with the individual. This personal muneedoo would be a patron to his assigned person for life.

Most muneedoos were good most of the time but could at times be mischievous or even spiteful. Nanabozho was a good example of this characteristic and the Ojibwa world was full of stories of this muneedoo. Examples of these stories are further illustrated in the section Gatherings, Games and Stories. Some of these muneedoos were evil. The evilest of all of them was matchi-muneedoo or the evil spirit. He is often compared with Satan of the Judeo-Christian world. One of the evil muneedoos that the Ojibwa feared the most was the Windego. The Ojibwa understanding of the relationship between the corporeal world and the spiritual realm allowed for crossover. An Anishinabe could become a spirit being. This explains the origin of the Windego.

The Windigo was a giant. It towered over the average man being eight to ten feet tall and its long strides made it possible for it to outrun even the swiftest Ojibwa. Its grey, putrid skin gave it a telltale rancid odour. It was pulled tight over its skeleton and its eyes were sunken giving it a grotesque appearance. This monster was a cannibal. It suffered from an insatiable hunger for human flesh. The more of it ate the hungrier it became. Its only objective was to try to satisfy its insatiable desire. Yet it was anaemic due to its perpetual starvation, as its food had no nutritional value.

In Ojibwa lore, the Windego represented one of the more despicable of human traits, greed. Each individual in Ojibwa society was expected to be giving toward the community in all areas. Sharing was required for the community to survive and if for example, winter supplies ran out and the people faced starvation then all faced it together. Sometimes human greed would surface and an individual would horde to the determent of others. This greedy person could suffer one of two fates. Either he or she could be turned into a Windigo or be eaten by one. The following is an Ojibwa legend about one person that became a Windego.

One particular summer drought had visited the territory of a certain Ojibwa band. The berries did not ripen so there was no harvest and game became very scarce. The following winter hunters returned to their hunting camps empty-handed too many times. The people were reduced to eating roots and tree bark trying to survive.

One individual's thoughts turned from the survival of the group to his own. He decided to visit a shaman to ask him for a talisman that would enable him to find food for himself. The shaman gave him some powder made from certain plant roots and told him to make a tea of it. After he drank it in secret he would be able to find food for himself. So, he awoke the next morning before anyone else made the tea and drank it.

Surprisingly he immediately began to grow. Taller and taller until he was twice the height of an ordinary man. And such long strides he had. He could cover great distances in so short a time and he could outrun even the swiftest of deer. Over the hills, his long strides carried him far away from his families hunting camp. He reached the top of a certain hill where he could see a village belonging to a different band of Ojibwa in a valley. He was so excited to see more prosperous people that he began to shout and run toward the village. However, his voice was deep and loud like the crack of thunder directly overhead. He was an awesome sight thundering and bounding down the hillside at twice the speed of a full-grown buck. The people of the village were so frightened that many of them dropped dead in their tracks. The others fled.

In next to no time he entered the village where there were plenty of provisions. He was famished but he had no craving for dried fruit, fish and venison. Instead, the aroma of the dead bodies that lay strewn on the ground instilled in him an eerie desire for human flesh. He began to taste some and soon devoured the whole body. But it was not enough. He was still starving so he began to eat more of the dead people and the more he ate the hungrier he became. The tea along with his own selfish greed had turned him into a Windigo!

Soon one of the village's most renowned warriors returned to the empty village. He was filled with grief when he discovered what had happened but his grief soon turned to rage. With all of his people gone he had nothing left but revenge and he set out on the trail of the Windego. With great determination he soon overtook him. The Windigo was in his habitual weakened state and begged for mercy but the warrior had none. In a rage, he killed the Windigo on the spot leaving his corpse as carrion for the vultures and crows.

Ojibwa cultural lore was filled with stories of Windigos. Each community had their own but all had the same morals to teach about generosity, greed, moderation and excesses.

The Ojibwa belief system revolved around their secret medicine society called the Midéwiwin Medicine Society or The Grand Medicine Society. Sometimes it was just referred to as "The Lodge". It was secret only in the sense that the multitude of medicines used for curing and divining and each individual chant that went with them was knowledge acquired by lodge members only through a long and arduous training program. Individuals were usually chosen as young children or adolescents according to a natural ability seen in them. They then would be initiated as trainees in an initiation ceremony. When they became the age to seek their vision, if they were boys, they would then be assigned a tutor. Girls were not required to seek their vision although they could if they wished. For an eyewitness account of a Midéwiwin initiation ceremony recorded by James Evans, Wesleyan missionary to the St. Clair Ojibwa, see appendix 5.

There were four orders in the hierarchy of the Lodge called degrees. After an initiate went through his or her initial training, which would take a year they became a candidate for First Degree Midéwiwin shaman or priest. After purifying himself in a sweat lodge ceremony he would undergo another Midéwiwin ceremony held in a specially constructed lodge called the Medéwigun. It was built the shape of a rectangle about 50 feet long by 25 feet wide facing east and west. It was open on the top and had a doorway at each end. A freshly cut cedar post called a Medéwitik stood inside the lodge and near it, a fire would be built. This ceremony accepted the candidate as a First Degree shaman. As an accredited First Degree he would now have the right to paint one bar on his face and preside at funerals and Feast of the Dead. Sometime after the ceremony, when the candidate was ready, he had to declare his intention of seeking the next level before he could go on. These steps were repeated for each degree with some changes in the actual liturgy of each and in the privileges acquired by the candidates. After a member completed his Fourth Degree training and ceremony he was accredited as a Fourth Degree Midéwiwin Priest and would follow his vocation as either diviner or healer. He would still, however, have to attend one Midéwiwin ceremony each year for renewal.[77]

The spiritual realm and the physical realm were often connected through the practice of medicine. Medicine was not practised as it is today. Medicine was a part of religion and it was the shaman that had the responsibility of serving his community with healing as well as communion with the spirit world. There were two types of the shaman in the Midéwiwin Lodge, the healing shaman and the divining shaman. Sometimes these medicine men were called jugglers and conjurors respectively.

The healing shaman, called nanandawi, had a catalogue of cures for various ailments made up of the right mixtures of herbs and plants. Of course for the healing power to be released these mixtures had to be invoked with the right ceremonies and chants. Healing shamen were commonly called tube suckers after the type of rituals practised by them. If a person became sick the healing shaman would visit him alone in the privacy of his lodge. After ascertaining where in the body the ailment was he would take out his paraphernalia consisting of a bowl, three or four hollowed out bones about the size of a child's finger and a rattle. He would begin by chanting to the cadence of his rattle with this ritual gaining all the while in boisterous sounds. This was done to invoke his personal muneedoo who would instruct him as to the exact nature of the ailment and the proper medicines to use. He would then take one of the bones called tubes and place one end on the person's body where the sickness was believed to reside. The shaman would then suck on the tube and spit the infection in the bowl. He would repeat this ritual until the bile contained little or no blood. Meanwhile, outside of the lodge, other members of the village would support the shaman by drumming and chanting for their own muneedoos to aid in the healing. The following records the healing of a Wisconsin Ojibwa youth by a traditional shaman named Old Man Hay using the tube sucking ritual. The testimony is of the youth whose name was Tom Badger who was suffering severe pains in his side.

In the evening Old Man Hay started to doctor me. He used those bones to doctor me. First, he told me to lay on my left side. Then he put the bone right on the place where my pain was. He put his head down

---

77 For a complete description of the *Medewiwin* Lodge and its ceremonies see Johnston, Basil. *Ojibway Heritage*, Toronto: McClelland and Stewart, 1994, 80-93.

close and kept pushing as hard as he could on that bone. When he put the bone away finally, the skin pulled back. That's when it hurt most of all. He started twice to doctor me. The second time he did the same thing he did the first time. When a sucking doctor starts to cure, he first tells the people there about the dream he had at the time he was fasting. Old Man Hay did that. Then my father beat a War Dance drum. Old Man Hay shook a rattle while he doctored me. He put a little dish next to him, with a little water in it. The two bones were lying there. They were about one and a half to two inches long. He didn't touch them with his hands but picked them up with his mouth. He didn't even have to pick them up with his mouth. His power was so strong that when Old Man Hay leaned over the dish, the bones stood up and moved towards his mouth. He swallowed the bones twice and coughed them up again. Then he put the bone to my side. After he'd finished sucking, Old Man Hay drew out some stuff and spat it into a dish; it looked like blood. Old Man Hay showed it to me and to the others and then threw it into the fire. If he hadn't draw the blood out it would have turned to pus. And sometimes, when the pus burst inside, the person dies. My father drummed all the time that Old Man Hay was doctoring me. He didn't sing, but Old Man Hay sang a little bit at the beginning of every time he doctored me. He put the bone to my side four times and got blood each time, but the last time he doctored me there was very little blood. It was the same every time he doctored me. All we gave him was a piece of cloth and some tobacco and gave him his meals. After he had finished doctoring me, Old Man Hay said to my father, "One time they had a medicine dance. You took the hide that Tom got in the medicine dance and gave it to someone else. You promised to give him another one in place of the one you took from him. Sometimes he thinks about it. That's why he is sick now."[78]

The divining shaman, called jiiskiiwnini, communed with the muneedoos while in a trance state. He did this while in a small lodge, called a jiiskaan, specifically constructed for this purpose. This lodge is commonly called a shaking tent and the jiiskiiwnini a shaker. He would perform this ceremony in order to divine some information that remained hidden. For example, an individual or a community might call for a shaker to help find something or someone who was lost. The shaker

---

78 Grim, John A. *The Shaman*. Norman, OK: University of Oklahoma Press, 1983, 107-08.

would perform the shaking tent ceremony to elicit information on the location of the lost item or person. The ceremony was performed in the following manner.

The shaker would prepare himself for the ceremony either by purifying himself in a sweat lodge, make an offering to his personal muneedoo or smoke some sacred tobacco. The purpose of this preliminary rite was to induce a dream validation in which he would be given the proper symbols to chant and their meaning. These were inscribed on a piece of birch bark and kept. Only he understood the meaning of the symbols and the proper words to chant for each one. This invocation chant would be performed in order to prepare the shaker for the shaking tent ceremony. First, his own spirit patron would be invoked and he would undergo an inner transformation that allowed him to be an intermediary figure himself. He then would consciously relate this transformation to the Midéwiwin Lodge so as not to personalize it, which would distort the spiritual power that had entered him. He would now be ready to bring together this power with his traditional mystical knowledge in the shaking tent ceremony he was about to perform.

Meanwhile, his assistants would construct a shaking tent by inserting four poles into the ground supported by four crosspieces tied about 2 feet intervals up the vertical poles. One of the vertical posts is higher than the other three by a couple of feet and had the branched left on the top. The wood used to construct the lodge was usually pine. The pine needles at the top of the higher post acted as a conduit for the muneedoos to enter the shaking tent. The top of the lodge was left open but the sides were covered with bark except for a small door through which the shaker entered the tent. A string of bells was sometimes tied between two of the posts.

After dusk when the spiritual readiness of both the shaker and the spiritual world converged the shaker entered the tent and began to drum. There may be drumming also done by the villagers. This was done to induce a trance state in the shaker and to summon the muneedoos into the tent. When they arrived the tent would begin to shake and all drumming would cease. Multiple voices and sparks of light coming from within the tent would also confirm their presence. The shaker would respond to questions from the villagers outside the tent by interpreting the muneedoos' words, which would be spoken in archaic Ojibwa. The shaker using this ceremony would ascertain the location of the lost item or person.

CHAPTER 14

Death Customs

There were two ceremonies performed by the Midéwiwin shaman, the funeral rite and the Feast of the Dead. Sometimes, if the person was on the brink of death, the funeral rite was begun before the sick or the injured person died. If this were the case the family would take care to dress the person in his or her finest clothing. Their hair would be impeccably fixed and adorned with feathers. Their personal belongings would be laid out beside them. These would include all the items that person would have used in daily life. If the person were a warrior they would include his war club, knife, musket, ball and shot, flint and tinder, his finest blanket, his pipe and tobacco, a bowl and spoon and his medicine pouch. If the dying person were a woman they would place beside her medicine bag, blanket, comb, flint and tinder, cooking utensils, bowl and spoon and sewing gear. These items would be needed for the long journey on the Path of Souls. This led to the Land of Souls where they would be reunited with their loved ones and friends that had gone on before them. This place was believed to be located somewhere in the west and was a place of peace and plenty. As the person lie dying the shaman would chant with the cadence of his rattle continuously keeping any evil muneedoo away. The women attending would wail and moan loudly when the person was unconscious, but if that person regained consciousness they would stop. The men did not mourn out loud.

If the person were a warrior, he would be placed in the sitting position at or just after death, as this was the position he would be buried in. The shaman would speak to the soul of the dead person by chanting instructions while the soul undergoes a change in essence to spirit. He would then leave for a time but the mourners would stay with the body lamenting all the time except for a few of the men who would go off to dig the grave, which would only be four or five feet deep.

When the grave was readied the men would return to join the lamentations. Eventually, the shaman would return and chant instructions to the spirit to prepare him for his four-day journey to the Land of Souls. These instructions would include warnings of the dangers to expect on the journey. He would then relate to the people the stories of the origins of the ceremonies, stories of the Path of Souls and stories of the Land of Souls. When he was finished the internment would begin the next morning. The family of the deceased would gather all manner of gifts such as grain, pelts, and other trade goods and place them near the grave.

The Ojibwa used four pallbearers who would carry the bark-encased body to the gravesite. The shaman, the women attendants and all the mourners would accompany them. A fire would be lit and kept going for four days. The body would be placed in the grave facing west with his or her possessions at their feet. The shaman would chant a hymn of benediction and the men would fill the grave with earth. A grave post would be planted at the head of the grave with the person's totem etched on it and perhaps some other markings representing extraordinary deeds. A small grave house made of bark would be constructed over the grave about 30 inches high and the length of the grave. It would have a small entrance on the west end of the house for the spirit of the deceased to exit to the Path of Souls. The gifts brought earlier were moved to the front of the grave house and the women would light a small fire. The mourners would all sit in a circle and during this vigil, some of the relatives and close friends would stand and give a eulogy when they felt the need to do so. This continued for four days with attendants tending the grave and keeping the fire going. At the end of the fourth day the shaman, attendants, and gravediggers would be paid in trade goods. The deceased's soul having completed its transformation to spirit could now begin the long journey to the Land of Souls.

While this journey took place a period of celebration would commence with one of the men stepping forward with a small stick in his hand. He would toss it to the crowd and all would try to catch it. One would but the others would try to wrestle it away from him. This continued until all or most had handled the stick and when one finally held fast to the stick he would be awarded some prize. It then would be announced that another prize would be awarded to the winner of a footrace. All the young men line themselves in a single line across the start and race on a predetermined course to the designated finish line.

After these celebratory activities, the people would return to the village where the relatives would give a feast for all mourners that were not relatives nor related by marriage. They were informed that the deceased was providing for the feast and a small piece of food from this feast must be taken by the guests and placed at the grave. They then returned to the village where they could eat as much as they want and they were also allowed to take the rest of their portions home with them. The guests of the feast are then given considerable presents, thanked and congratulated on their own generosity.

The widow or widower would enter a period of mourning that would last for one year. If a widow she would move into the lodge of her husband's parents for the mourning period. She would wear her hair down and unbraided. She replaced her good dress with an old worn one and she would wear a sash over her left shoulder and tied at her right hip. Her good dress folded and placed in a birch bark pouch, which was tied to her waist. Any gifts she received during the mourning period would be added to this bundle. She was required to attend her husband's grave every a day until released from the mourning period. At the end of the year, she would ask her husband's parents to release her from her outward mourning after which she would replace the worn dress with her good one, be able to use the gifts held in her birch bark pouch and would be free to remarry.

The living was responsible for the care of the dead. The graves were tended regularly during a three-year cycle, but at the end of the cycle, a Feast of the Dead would be held. At this time a special lodge would be built about 120 feet long, open on the top and with several tiers running along the insides of it. It would be constructed using fresh bark only and have three long poles planted one at each end and a taller one in the centre. They would be painted and greased and have a prize attached to the top each of them. The prize would belong to the first person to be able to scale the pole and touch the prize.

After this contest each family would disinter the bodies of their relatives, clean the bones and place them in birch bark containers bringing them to a lodge and placing them on the ledges. They then heaped all the gifts they had collected during the three years on the remains. With faces painted black, they would partake of a great feast, which they would leave occasionally returning to the lodge where they would circle making a great noise by shooting muskets in the air and bellowing loud whoops. They would then return to the feast to eat some more. Back and forth the mourners would go all the while making a din of noise for three days and three nights. At the end of this time, the relatives would retrieve the gifts from the lodge and distributed them to the guests that were not relatives.

They then retrieve the bones from the lodge after which the men circled the lodge one more time shouting their mourning whoops and striking the structure with large poles knocking it to pieces. At the same time, the women threw bundles of kindling on the collapsed lodge and it was burned. As an anti-climax, a Dog Feast was held where a great number of dogs were killed and feasted upon. Dogs were highly regarded by the village and deemed appropriate as a sacrifice to offer up prayers for the dead. After the Dog Feast, the relatives took the bones to a desolate place where they were hidden in hollows or between rocks. The dead were never spoken of again. This was the climax of the Feast of the Dead and served as final closure for the living.

CHAPTER 15

Band Designations, Totems and Wampum

Each Band had its own hunting territory and these territories were given their own appellations to identify them. Some examples of these were given in the above section on the Iroquois War. The Bawitigwakinini, for example, was one of the better-known bands. This is only because of their location, which was around the Falls of St. Mary's at Sault Ste. Marie. Bawitig means falls or rapids and inini denotes man. When given the prefix wak it means people or more literally men. This word translates as People of the Falls. The Mississauga or Eagle People were located south of the Bawitigwakinini on the north shore of Georgian Bay. Amikwa were known as the Beaver People, Amik meaning Beaver. They were located south of the Mississauga.[79] Ketchesebewininewug were the Great River Men because they lived on the Banks of the Mississippi River.[80] As can be seen, by this abbreviated list some of these bands had some animal either mammal, fish, bird or reptile embedded in their names and some had some other feature. This is because the names give some clue as to the location of the band's hunting territory for example whether they lived near great rapids or good beaver hunting territory.

---

79 For a complete list of locations of Ojibwa Bands see Thwaites, Ruben Gold, *The Jesuit Relations and Allied Documents*, Vol. XVIII, 227-235.

80 Warren, 39. Warren provides a complete list of Ojibway Bands located in the United States.

Band appellations can be very confusing when trying to trace band movements. These names could change or even disappear which often happened when bands relocated. Or they sometimes took their names with them. Sometimes they changed their band's name to describe some feature of their new location. For example, when a part of the Bawitigwakinini relocated to Southeast Michigan they split into two bands. One band called themselves Mekadewagamitigwayawininiwak or Men at the end of the Black River. The other Band called themselves Wapisiwisibwininiwak or Men of Swan Creek. Yet the French still referred to them as Sauteurs. When the Amikwa moved south of Georgian Bay the band that moved into Saugeen Territory became know as Saugeewinini meaning "I am of the People of the River Mouth".[81]

These band names were in full use during the seventeenth century but fell out of use by the European record keepers during the eighteenth century. When the British became the dominant European power after defeating the French at Quebec in 1760 they ceased using the old appellations altogether referring to the Ojibwa as Chippewa. However, Ojibwa Bands still use some descriptive appellation even today. For example, Aamjiwnaang njibaad meaning I am from a place where the waters run contrary (Sarnia) or Bkejwanong njibaad meaning I am from a place where the waters divide (Walpole Island).

There are two essential questions in Ojibwa culture when introductions are made between strangers. The first one is "Waenaesh keen?" meaning who are you? The answer provided would be one of band membership such as the examples above. But, the premier question and the one always asked first is "Waenaesh k'dodaem" meaning what is your totem.[82] Totems were family marks. They were almost always a pictogram of an animal, either a mammal, bird, fish or reptile and denoted which family an individual belonged to. During the surrender treaty period, chiefs and principal men of the different bands used totems as a sign of their speaking authority for their families. The chiefs would make their totem mark on the document and the government would write their personal names phonetically beside their marks.

---

81 Johnson, Basil. *Ojibway History*, McClelland and Stewart, Toronto: 1974, 59-60.

82 Ibid. 59.

According to tradition, in the beginning, there were only five totems and they were a gift from the spirit beings. Warren relates the traditional story this way:

When the earth was new, the An-ish-in-aub-ag lived, congregated on the shores of a great salt water. From the bosom of the great deep, there suddenly appeared six beings in human form who entered their wigwams.

One of these six strangers kept a covering over his eyes, and he dared not look on the An-ish-in-aub-ag, though he showed the greatest anxiety to do so. At last, he could no longer restrain his curiosity, and on one occasion he partially lifted his veil, and his eye fell on the form of a human being, who instantly fell dead as if struck by one of the thunderers. Though the intentions of this dread being were friendly to the An-ish-in-aub-eg, yet the glance of his eye was too strong and inflicted certain death. His fellows, therefore, caused him to return into the bosom of the great water from which they had apparently emerged.

The others, who now numbered five, remained with the An-ish-in-aub-eg and became a blessing to them; from them originate the five great clans or Totems, which are known among the Ojibways by the general terms of A-Wause-e, Bus-in-aus-e, Ah-ah-wauk, Noka, and Monsone or Waub-ish-ash-e. These are cognomens which are used only in connection with the Totemic system.[83]

Some researchers confuse band designations with totems because often band designations have some animal or bird rooted in the band name. Sometimes clans are referred to but totems are strictly family marks. Some of the different families may be more closely related and Warren mentions this calling them great families. He gives the example of some of the smaller fish totems being closely related or belonging to one of the largest families, the Awause family, who claim the Meshemunaigway (immense fish) as their totem.[84]

I personally do not like the word clan because it evokes a western mentality producing the concept of a hierarchical societal structure such as nations made up of tribes made up of clans, who are made up of families. European clans have a coat of arms and keep strict track of family branches. Clan members could be related either closely or distantly. Distant relatives could marry even if they were of the same clan.

---

83 Warren, *History*, 44

84 Ibid. 46.

Some have taken this model and tried to superimpose it on Ojibwa society. But, Ojibwa society was very flatly organized. Families were the backbone of the nation with each family represented in many bands. This, along with a common language, is what held the Ojibwa together. Individuals with the same totem, no matter how remote the bands were to each other and even if they did not know each other, were considered close relatives. No member of the same totem was a distant relation. They used close relative names such as sister for sister-in-law and brother for brother-in-law. Totems were used in the marriage tradition to prevent intermarriage. It was a highly immoral act to marry one from the same totem even if they were only remotely blood-related. Because of the flat societal organization and the principle that there are only close relatives I believe the European Clan system does not fit Ojibwa society. See Appendix 6 for a visual flowchart of the two systems.

Families were expected to be responsible for visiting members of the same totem, even if they were strangers as if they were brothers or sisters providing them with both food and shelter. Totems were inherited and could not be changed. They were patrilineal so the children of the marriage would carry their father's totem, however, the mother kept her totem.

I intimated earlier that there were totems of objects other than animals. One such example is my own totem. My father writes of his father Zaagmshkodewe "... my father's totem is oak."[85] Zaagmshkodewe's grandfather Animikince, both a war chief and a civil chief, signed several American treaties including the Peace Treaty of Greenville, the Treaty of Detroit and several British treaties including Treaties 6, 7 and 29. Invariably researchers have interpreted his totem as "an antler totem" or "caribou". But, his mark represented a tree, the mighty oak. Also, one of the signatories of Treaty 20 was "Pininse, of the White Oak Tribe".[86] These are examples of totems of trees. Trigger and Day mention a "Birch bark" totem as well.[87] Some other examples, although not Ojibwa are a

---

85 Plain, Nicholas, *The History of the Chippewa's of Sarnia and the History of the Sarnia Reserve*, s.l, Sarnia, ON: 1951, 4.

86 *Indian Treaties and Surrenders*, vol. 1, Coles Publishing Company, Toronto: 1992, 48.

87 Trigger, Bruce G. and Gordon M. Day, "Southern Algonquin Middlemen", *Aboriginal Ontario*, 144.

notched arrow of the Illinois, a big stone or rock of the Assinipoëls and the Flatheads had a vessel as a totem.[88]

Each individual had a personal name. An elder of the band usually named the child during a naming ceremony. More often than not personal names are based on a dream, vision or an event and may not be given for up to two years. A personal name could be changed. For example, a man might wish to honour his late father and so take his name for himself. Personal names were not used as signatory devices or in introductions. In fact, during everyday communications, a nickname, usually given during the person's youth, was preferred. For a list of some personal names along with some biographical information see Appendix 7.

First Nations societies were oral societies. Because they had no written language they used wampum to seal treaties and other agreements. Wampum was usually a belt of beads with designs or pictograms on them but could be other objects such as a calumet, strings of beads, or an animal pelt. A speaker in council would hold up the wampum explaining what it represented and the acceptance of this wampum by the other party constituted a contract that remained in force until the wampum was surrendered to the party giving it. These contracts were held in the highest esteem and never broken, as it would have been a highly dishonourable thing to break one's word. Sir Francis Bond Head understood this truth and confirmed it in correspondence written by him to Lord Glenelg regarding his removal policy and dated 20th November 1836.

It will be asked, in what way were these promises made; − it is difficult to reply to this question, as it involves the character of the Indian race.

An Indian's word, when it is formally pledged, is one of the strongest moral securities upon earth: like the rainbow, it beams unbroken, when all beneath is threatened with annihilation.

The most solemn form in which an Indian pledges his word is by the delivery of a wampum belt of shells and when the purport of this symbol

---

88 See "Enumeration of the Indian Tribes ... 1736, Collections of the State Historical Society of Wisconsin, vol. 17, 245-252.

is once declared, it is remembered and handed down from father to son with an accuracy and retention of memory which is quite extraordinary.[89]

The Iroquois War ended with a general peace treaty signed in Montreal in 1701. The Five Nation Confederacy secured a further peace with the Three Fires Confederacy at a council held at Lake Superior by delivering a wampum belt. Each generation was charged with renewing the peace by taking out the belt at a council and remembering the meaning of its symbols. In 1840 Ojibwa chief Yellowhead read the belt at a Renewal Council, which was attended by the Iroquois. See Yellowhead's speech in appendix 8 for a description of the belt and the meaning of its symbols.

After the Royal Proclamation of 1763, some 1500 First Nations chiefs and warriors including those of Saugeen Territory met with Sir William Johnson at Niagara Falls. The purpose of the council was to secure a peace after Pontiac's War. They met in July 1764 and Johnson presented the First Nations with two wampum belts. Of the first belt (see fig. 1) he said, "My children, I clothe your land, you see that Wampum before me, the body of my words, in this spirit of my words shall remain, it shall never be removed, this will be your Mat the eastern Corner of which I myself will occupy, the Indians being my adopted children their life shall never sink in poverty."

By these words, he was in agreement with the First Nations that the British recognized the ownership of the land and that they would respect that by only occupying the eastern corner of it leaving the rest for the First Nations to prosper in as allies.

Figure 1

The second wampum presented by Johnson was called the twenty-four-nation belt (see fig. 2.). The twenty-four figures represented the twenty-four First Nations of the covenant pulling a British ship laden with presents. This wampum symbolized the following words of the

---

89 *Report of the Indians of Upper Canada by a Sub-Committee* printed for The Aborigines Protection Society, William Ball, Arnold and Co., London: 1839, 20.

British, "My children, wee, this is my Canoe floating on the other side of the Great Waters, it shall never be exhausted but always full of the necessities of life for you my Children as long as the world shall last.

Should it happen anytime after this that you find the strength of your life reduced, your Indian Tribes must take hold of the Vessel and pull, it shall be all in your power to pull towards you this my Canoe, and where you have brought it over to this Land on which you stand, I will open my hand as it were, and you will find yourselves supplied with plenty."

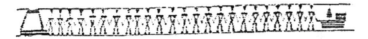

Figure 2

Unfortunately, although the Europeans understood the solemness of wampum they did not follow through, as their words did not last.[90]

---

90 Johnston, Darlene. *Connecting People to Place: Great Lakes Aboriginal History in Cultural Context*, prepared for The Ipperwash Inquiry, 14,15.

CHAPTER 16

Shelter

In warm weather, the cone-shaped tepee was used and not a great deal of attention was paid to its construction. Several straight saplings were cut about twelve feet long and about 2 inches in diameter at the butt end and 1 inch at the tip. Twelve poles would make a tepee of about ten feet in diameter. 2 of these were fixed firmly in the ground, then crossed at a height of about six feet where they were tied with strips of basswood bark. A third pole was then leaned on the other two where they crossed and it was also tied securely. After this, the rest of the poles were laid on the cross of the structure sloping to the ground and cedar bark was laid upon the framework leaving a hole at the top to let out any smoke from cooking fires that may have to be used during inclement weather. This was a temporary dwelling used only as shelter from gentle summer rains and for sleeping in. At night a fire was built in the centre of the tepee in a smudge pot with green wood and leaves to make smoke. The hole at the top could be closed off with a piece of bark if need be. The smoke rose in the tepee leaving about two feet clear on the floor where the people slept. The purpose of the smoke was to ward off mosquitoes.

During the winter months, more attention was given to the construction of the wigwam. It was dome shaped and its footprint was either circular or oblong. Poles similar to the wigwam poles, but about 1½ inch in diameter at the butt end, were cut and planted into the ground 1 foot deep and eighteen inches apart. Enough poles were cut to encircle the base, which was about twelve feet in diameter. This size would have housed a family of two. The vertical poles were then bent inward toward the centre and tied. Cross poles were then tied to the sides for support.

They could be smaller than the vertical poles about 1 inch at the butt end. The butt end was tied first and worked toward the tip. They were tied approximately 2 feet apart up to the top. A hole was left for the doorway, which could be closed off by hanging a blanket over it or with birch bark pinned to a frame. If the shape was oblong then a doorway was left at each end. The door was about 6 inches bigger than the opening all the way around. A smoke hole was left in the very centre of the top. The covering was pinned with large thorns. The wigwam was insulated first with woven mats, then cedar boughs and earth and finally covered with snow.

Bunks were built along the sides about eighteen inches high to sit or sleep on. Two-inch poles with forks at the top end were used for vertical posts tying the horizontal poles to the forks. Sticks ½ inch to ¾ inch were tied to the horizontal side rails for the bed. Cedar boughs were spread on top of the sticks for comfort.

A fire pit was made in the centre of the wigwam by laying large stones in a rectangle about 1 ½ foot wide by 2 foot long. The stones were buried halfway in the ground. Two poles about 3 ½ feet long were planted a foot deep at each end of the pit. These had a fork on the top end to lay a pole across for cooking. Fresh meat or fish was laid over the cooking pole. Utensils such as brooms and birch bark or reed baskets and were made for use around the wigwam.

The wigwam was very warm and comfortable even in the coldest of winter nights as reported by Major Strickland in the mid-nineteenth century. "The Indian wigwams are very warm. I have slept in them in the coldest weather with only one blanket wrapped about me, without experiencing the least inconvenience arising from either draft or cold.[91]

---

91 Strickland, *Twenty-seven*, vol. II, 34.

CHAPTER 17

Agriculture and Gathering

The Ojibwa did not engage in a lot of agriculture. Small garden plots were cultivated during the summer months when the band was congregated at the main village. It fell to the women and children to tend these gardens. Indian corn and pumpkin were the main crops and were only grown to supplement the band's food supply. Most of the foodstuffs were hunted, fished or gathered for. The following are some of the fruits and nuts gathered and how they were processed. This work also fell to the women and children.

Wild plums were gathered in October. They were plentiful and grew mainly along the shoreline of rivers and small lakes. Some of this crop was boiled with sugar and would fill the air with a light forest aroma. Sometimes they would be dried but mostly they would be boiled with maple sugar and made into a kind of cake dough. The plums would be boiled in a pot and stirred until the mass became thick, then spread out on a piece of hide or birch bark to the thickness of about one inch and dried in the sun. Once dry it forms a tough solid substance and it is rolled up and stored in birch bark boxes. They are stored in a hole in the ground, covered with earth and stored for the winter. During the winter months, if there was no fresh meat, pieces of this substance were cut off and boiled with dried meat. Taking a couple of handfuls of shredded, dried meat and some wild plumbs and blueberries and boiling the mixture made venison soup.

No salt was used in traditional cooking. Maple sugar was used in preparing their meat as well as being sprinkled over fish boiled in water.

Maple sugar was also used as a treat, which the children loved to eat piece by piece.

The wild cherry was also very common. Commonly called "sand cherries" they ripen in August. The women collected them at the same time as the blueberries and were prepared in various ways. One way was to crush the cherries between two rocks then mixing them with the fat of the deer and boiling the mixture until it forms a dough. This is also stored in birch bark boxes as a winter supply. Small red apples were also harvested from the wild apple trees dried and eaten as a desert.

Blueberries and blackberries were also gathered and highly prized as a crop. They were usually dried by laying them out on frames of white wood and hung over a slow fire. When quite dry they were packed in birch bark boxes and later mixed with the bread dough. The sweet tasting berries were also boiled with fish or meat and would substitute for sugar late in the winter season if the sugar ran out.

Another berry of great value to the Ojibwa was the wild cranberry. They were bittersweet tasting berries yet pleasant and refreshing. They grew in swampy areas and ripened in October. These berries did not require drying, as they would last the whole winter without spoiling.

Wild hazelnuts were also collected and kept in bags. They were used in place of butter often being eaten with their bread. Pounded nuts would also give the unsalted cornbread a delicious flavour. When there was neither nuts nor fat to take off the blandness of the cornbread a decoction of ashes was used. Warm water would be poured over the ashes from white wood. The course part would fall to the bottom. Then the ash water would be filtered and the ash water would be poured on the dough. This ash water was also used in making soup. Indian corn was also soaked in the water as part of its preparation process.

One of the roots used by the Ojibwa for food was known as the swan potato. These grew in the water, on the banks of rivers and lakes. They were gathered and threaded on strings of white wood and then hung in the lodge to be smoked. They were very small when dried, but swelled out when boiled. They were considered better than regular potatoes, very sweet and soft. Another root highly prized was the spruce root. It was a long, thin, knotty root light brown in colour, which was boiled and tasted like watercress. They were also dried and pounded between two stones into powder, which was used like flour to make bread. This powder could also be used to make soup by making a thin broth and adding any edible grain or pea or bean to it. Wild carrots were also boiled as a vegetable and tasted like the domestic carrot only stronger.

Several fresh herbs were also gathered and eaten fresh. One such herb used in cooking was the trout herb. The leaves were collected in the spring when young and they were called the leaves of the trout. They were used to make a very tasty and nutritious green fish soup. Even the bones and offal of the fish were used. They were pounded between stones then boiled with the trout herbs.[92]

---

92 Kohl, J.G., *Kitchi-Gami*, 318-22. Also see Letitia Root, *Through the Eyes of the Elders*, M&T Printing Service for Saugeen Community Remedial Outreach for Learning Literacy 1996, for a complete description for making traditional scone and corn soup.

CHAPTER 18

Trade

A report on the American Colonies to King George I written on the 8th of September 1721 stated that, "From the north east of the Lake Erie to a fort on the lake St. Clair, called fort Chartrim, [Pontchartrain] is about eight leagues sail; here the french have a settlement, and often 400 traders meet there along this Lake they proceed about seven leagues further, and thence to the great Lake Huron about ten leagues; hence they proceed to the straits of Michilimackinack 120 leagues. Here is a garrison of about 30 french, and a vast concourse of traders, sometimes not less than 1,000, besides Indians, being a common place of rendezvous. At and near this place the Outawas an Indian nation are settled."[93]

Undoubtedly the Saugeen Ojibwa would have traded either at Michilimackinac or Detroit. They also wanted to trade at Albany with the British and would travel that far if the goods were much cheaper. British goods were also known to be of better quality than French goods. In "An Abridgment of the Indian Affairs" on June 28th 1729 regarding trade with the far Indians it was reported "The Commissrs receive them very friendly & give them Assurances of Protection & good usage in Trade & tell them that they will find they can buy at Albany more for One Bever than for 3 with the French".[94] Another manuscript reports:

It must not be forgotten, also, that with very few exceptions the Indian tribes of the west remained faithful to the cause of France until the end of the French domination in America. Frontenac, Denonville,

---

93 Michigan Pioneer and Historical Society, Vol. 19, 5.

94 Wraxall, Peter in: ***Harvard Historical Studies,*** vol. XXI, 177.

and other French officials had the same distrust of the Indians as Perrot; but the latter governor admitted that they were attracted to the English by the better market thus afforded for the sale of their peltries. As proof of this, is cited a Ms. dated 1689, in the archives of the Marine, showing the difference in prices at Orange [Albany] and Montreal; for one beaver-skin an Indian received at Orange forty pounds of lead, or a red blanket, or a large overcoat, or four shirts, or six pairs of hose, while at Montreal each of these items cost him two pelts, and even three for the above quantity of lead. A gun cost two pelts at Orange, and five at Montreal; and one pelt procured for the Indian eight pounds of gunpowder from the English, while the French demanded four for that quantity. "The other petty wares which the savages buy in trade from the French are given to them by the English as part of the bargain. The English give six pots of brandy for one beaver-skin; this is rum, or guildive (otherwise sugar-cane brandy), which they import from the islands of America [i.e., the West Indies]. The French have not standard [of price] for the brandy trade; some give more, and others less, but they never go so high as one pot for one beaver-skin... It is to be noted that the English make no difference as regards the quality of the beaver-skins, which they buy all at the same price— which is more than fifty per cent higher than the French give; and, besides, there is more than one hundred per cent difference in the value of their trade and that of ours."— Tailhan.[95]

The French did everything in their power to prevent any First Nations trade with the British. On the 14th of July 1724 the following was reported in An Abridgement of Indian Affairs made to the Governor of New York "14 July Several Far Indians arrive to Trade with Bever &[c] & say the French used every Artifice in their Power to prevent their coming to Albany & had by promises & Threatenings prevailed upon 30 Canoes of Indians to go to Canada who had never been at Albany & intended to have come with them hither".[96] Far Indians were First Nations from the Upper Great Lakes, mostly Ojibwa, which included the Saugeen Ojibwa.

---

95 Perrot, Nicolas: Memoir on the Manners, Customs and Religion of the Savages of North America, Leipzig and Paris, 1864, from n 181, Blair, *The Indian Tribes of the Upper Mississippi Valley and Regions of the Great Lakes*, Volume I, Cleveland, Ohio, 1911, 258.

96 Wraxall, *Harvard*, 152.

This trade activity like most travel was done using the birch bark canoe. This was a light, highly manoeuvrable vessel, yet it was extremely strong and able to carry very heavy loads. They were made of various lengths from fourteen feet for a family to thirty feet for trading or war. They were constructed in the following manner. First, the proper tree was selected. It was as large and smooth as possible to provide the largest sheets of bark. The larger the sheets the less sewing required. It should also have been free of any lichen growth, which may allow the bark to split under pressure. Also not forked at the top. Ideally, a single piece was needed the length of the canoe and wide enough to reach the gunwales at the centre of the canoe. Otherwise, pieces would have to be sown on to the sides in order to reach the gunwales. This piecing would have required double stitching.

The tree was either felled or the bark is taken from the tree while standing. Two incisions were made around the tree at each end then one vertical cut was made from top to bottom. The taking of the bark had to be done at the proper time of year, sometime in June. If the air temperatures were right the bark would pop off.

The construction site was chosen and a flat bed of sand free of rocks or twigs was spread out in a rectangular shape. A wigwam was built over the site to prevent any direct sunlight from drying out the materials too quickly and curling the bark. The bottom piece was spread out on the bed of sand with the outside or white side facing up. An oblong-shaped wooden canoe form with pointed ends was then placed on the bottom piece. The sides were then drawn up the length of the canoe and cedar steaks were driven into the ground along both sides of the canoe to enable the canoe to begin to take form. The ends of the piece of bark were then pinched together and held by cedar pins. The outer steaks were then tied together with strips of basswood bark. If the sides of the bark were not sufficient to reach the whole length of the gunwales then strips of bark needed to be double stitched onto the sides. Four long thin cedar gunwales were then put in place along the perimeter of the canoe two on each with the bark in between. The inner gunwales would have already been mortised to receive the three thwarts. These will keep the canoe from spreading. Once in place, the gunwales were lashed together the full length of each side of the canoe. The bow and stern were worked on next. Stems were made from cedar pieces about 1¾ inch wide 5/8 of an inch deep and 27 inches long. They would be split so the rings were running across the flatter part of the wood. Each stem piece was then split with a knife into 8 pieces for easier bending. The stems were bent into the proper shape by pouring boiling water over them to make them pliable, bending them into shape and tying them with basswood bark string so they would hold their shape. When dried they were placed inside the bow and stern and pegged temporarily into place. The gunwales were lashed together and the excess bark was then trimmed and sewn together. Either tamarack or cedar roots were used in the sewing.

Now the cedar ribs were bent into shape. They were soaked for several days in water to make them pliable and when they were to be shaped, boiling water was poured over them to make them even more pliable. About forty were cut about ½ inch thick and 2 inches wide for a fourteen-foot family canoe. While standing on them one at a time the ends were gradually pulled up until the proper bend was achieved. They were then inserted into the canoe in their proper place and left for a day to dry. They were then removed and cedar planking, pieces about 1/8 of an inch thick and 3 to 4 inches wide were laid on the bottom of the canoe for flooring. The flooring was held in place by reinserting the ribs. A gunwale cap was then installed and held in place by birchwood pegs to protect the lashing holding the gunwales together.

The canoe was then inverted for pitching. Pitch was made from spruce gum and deer tallow. The canoe was sealed with this mixture wherever the bark had been cut and sewn. A container of this pitch was carried by the canoeist for use in repairing during travel. Once the pitch was dry the canoe was ready for use. It would take three to five weeks to build a canoe taking into consideration the time to find the right tree and to prepare the site and paraphernalia needed for construction.

CHAPTER 19

Gatherings, Games and Stories

During the summer months and into early autumn traditional gatherings took place. These were huge gatherings lasting for days and were held at traditional gathering places like Bawitig (Sault Ste. Marie) or Manitoulin Island. Great quantities of fish, berries and meat were consumed at these gatherings and drumming and dancing were constant. Games were played not just for entertainment but also for wagering. Old acquaintances were renewed as well as military alliances. These gatherings served to strengthen the Ojibwa people keeping them one of the most powerful First Nations in the great lakes basin.

Some of the games played were games of chance such as the game of straws and a game of dice. These games were played between villages or bands and some had been known to wager all the village-owned only to lose it all. Even so, these losses never contributed to any animosity between opponents. Also, foot races were conducted throughout the gathering and were esteemed by all. Bougainville describes footraces being held at Detroit in 1757, "At Détroit foot races between the savages and the Canadians are as celebrated as horse races in England. They take place in the spring. Ordinarily there are live [sic] hundred savages present, sometimes as many, as fifteen hundred. The course is a half league, going and returning from Détroit to the village of the Poutéouatamis; the road is well made and wide. There are posts planted at the two extremities;

the wagers are very considerable, and consist of packages of peltries laid against French merchandise such as is in use among the savages.[97]

They also played a ball game called baagaadowe, which the French called lacrosse. Sabrevois describes the game of lacrosse as follows:

In summer they Play a great deal at la crosse, twenty or more on each side. Their bat [crosse] is a sort of small racket, and The ball with which they Play Is of very Heavy wood, a little larger than the balls we use in Tennis.1 When they Play, they Are entirely naked; they have only a breech-clout, and Shoes of deer-skin. Their bodies are painted all over with all Kinds of colours. There are some who paint their bodies with white clay, applying it to resemble silver lace sewed on all the seams of a coat; and, at a distance, one would take it for silver lace. They play for large Stuns, and often The prize Amounts to more than 800 Livres. They set up two goals and begin Their game midway between; one party drives The ball one way, and the other in the opposite direction, and those who can drive It to the goal are the winners. All this is very diverting and interesting to behold. Often one Village Plays against another, the poux against the outaouacs or the hurons, for very considerable prizes.[98]

The game of straws was described by Charlevoix as follows: "...the game was played in the cabbin of the chiefs, and in a sort of square over against it. These straws are small rushed of the thickness of a stalk of wheat and two fingers in length. They take up a parcel of these in their hand, which generally consists of two hundred and one, and always of an unequal number. After they have well stirred them, and making a thousand contortions of body and invoking the genii, they divide them, with a kind of awl or sharp bone into parcels of ten: each takes one at a venture, and he to whom the parcel with eleven in it falls gains a certain number of points according to the agreement; sixty or four score make a party."[99]

The game of dice is also described by Sabrevois as follows: "This dish game is as follows. Eight little balls, red or black on one side, and yellow or white on the other, are tossed on a dish. When he who has the dish

97 WHC, Vol. XVIII, 194.

98 WHC, xvi, 366-67. For full description of lacrosse, see *Jesuit Relations*, x, 185-187, 231, 326-328; xv, 179.

99 Charlevoix, P. de in: *Journal of a Voyage to North **America,*** vol. 2, London, 1761, 102.

tosses them so that seven of the same colour turn up, or all eight, he wins, and continues to play as long as he throws in this way; but when he throws otherwise, he or she with whom be Plays takes The dish and Plays in turn. In all these games they Play for large sums."[100]

Ojibwa society was an oral society and as such produces great stories and storytellers. Most of the stories were designed to teach some truth or moral and were used as a form of entertainment. Each village had an official storyteller who would entertain the whole village around a communal fire in the centre of the village during the warm summer months. During the winter these stories were used to pass the long winter evenings.

These evenings would be spent in the warm, cosy lodges with the adults entertaining all with traditional stories. There were hundreds of stories and in most the central character was Nanabozho. He was a being whose father was a muneedoo or spirit being and his mother was human. He was a caricature of human nature and often he would not be able to do the things he should or would do the things he should not. His character was flawed with the baser human characteristics. He would often stumble along in an almost comical way exhibiting the inner weakness that all human beings struggle with. He means well but his tendency to give into this inner weakness often turns his adventures into misadventures and his successes into failures. Some of the stories of Nanabozho were very long but most were short. The following is an example of one of these types of stories.

One day Nanabozho was walking in the woods when he came to a small lake. He spotted a flock of geese in the water and being hungry he thought one would make a good meal. But then he got greedy and thought he would like to cook and eat them all. He devised a plan to capture all the geese at once. He fashioned a long rope of elm bark and crept up to the water's edge. Slipping into the lake he swam up underwater, rope in hand, to the floating geese. He began tying the geese's feet together with the rope and when he had them all tied together he rose out of the water with a shout. The startled geese took off flying higher and higher with Nanabozho dangling from the end of the rope. Finally, his strength ran out and he let go of the rope while flying over woodland. He fell into a hollow tree where a bear was sleeping so he

---

100 WHC. Vol. Xvi, 369.

asked the bear to take him down out of the tree, which he did. His weight had pulled the flock of geese into the shape of a V and geese have been flying that way ever since.

Another example is the story of the little boy that was orphaned and had to live with his grandmother. Unfortunately, his grandmother was of a wicked nature and soon began to torment the little boy so he wished Nanabozho would turn him into a bird. Nanabozho granted him his wish and he flew up into a tree that was growing near the old woman's wigwam. He started to laugh and his grandmother begged him to come back but he would not. And so we still have the red-breasted robin hanging around near people's lodges.

CHAPTER 20

Hunting and Trapping Camps

One of the main sources of food for the Ojibwa was meat with the pelts being used for clothing and other items. After the traditional gatherings were held in the fall the main village broke up and individual families of up to three would strike out into their traditional hunting territories to set up their hunting and trapping camps. Wigwams would be constructed in a place that offered both shelter from wind and snow and a good water supply. The men would set out each day to hunt or tend trap lines returning each evening to the camp. The women would spend the day tending the camp, cooking and processing game.

Deer and bear were particularly plentiful in Saugeen Territory. Before the introduction of firearms, there were four different ways of hunting big game. The first was with a snare. Rope made of wild hemp would be used to snare even large game such as deer. When the deer was snared about the neck the rope would tighten. The more the deer struggled the less it could because the rope, winding itself around the neck, would choke the prey. The first half of the day was spent setting snares and the second half was spent driving the deer into the area where the snares had been set.

The second way was to take sharp spikes of wood and drive them into the ground just past a log on the deer trail. The deer would be unable to see the spikes and when jumping over the log would fall upon them killing them by piercing them through.

The third way was to chase the deer with dogs. In the summer they would be chased into the water where they could easily be disposed of. In the winter they would be chased into deep snow where they would tire quickly.

The fourth way of hunting deer was with bow and arrow. Bows were made of sufficient strength to be able to shoot an arrow through the side of a deer with no difficulty. In summer the hunter would wait near the shoreline of a lake or river where deer often go to feed on grass. In winter he would wait just off a deer trail where he was able to kill his game from a distance of up to fifty paces. Bows were generally made of well-seasoned ironwood, red cedar or hickory. The sharp point of the arrow was made of either bone or shell carved with barbed ends. Black bears were also hunted with bow and arrow. They were an easy game in winter as they could be found hibernating in dens or hollow logs. They were more numerous in years when fruit, berries and nuts were most plentiful.[101] These were the hunting methods used before contact and the advent of guns.

Trapping became more prevalent after the fur trade and European iron traps were used. But the Ojibwa also engaged in trapping before the fur trade. Snares and wooden box traps were used to trap smaller game such as rabbit, beaver, otter, marten, fisher and lynx. Often a hollow log would be used and they were most efficient after a heavy snowfall because the small game would have difficulty finding food. The back end of the trap would not be closed off with anything solid but with a net because the game liked to see where it is going. A trap door was fixed to the top of the log with leather hinges. A hole was also made in the top of the log. A cord was run from the door to a trigger inside the log. It would hold the trap door at a 45° angle from the ground. The trigger would be attached to the inside of the log about 2 inches off the floor. It would be a piece of flat wood about 6 inches long and 2 inches wide. This trigger would be notched at its midpoint, as would the side of the log. A catch, stick about 6 inches long, would also be notched at its midpoint and the cord would be tied taut at the notch. This catch would be placed in the notches on the trigger and the inside of the log. Corn or some dried fruit would be attached to the trigger. The weight of the animal on the trigger would release the catch and the weight of the trap door would cause it to fall closing the open end of the log.

Instead of using a log sometimes a box would be constructed of 1-inch saplings notched and tied together. A large rock would be tied to the top of the box. One end of the box would be held up at 45° with

---

101 Copway, *Indian Life*, 34-35, 37.

a trigger device. This trigger was made of 3 sticks ½ inch in diameter notched and with the bark left on. It was made in a figure four shape with the bait end extending to the centre of the upheld box. When the bait end was disturbed the whole device collapsed allowing the box to fall over the animal trapping it. The heavy rock would hold the box over the trapped animal.

CHAPTER 21

Sugar Camps

After wintering in small family hunting camps they would congregate at various sugar bushes in groups of six or so families. This gathering would take on an almost festival atmosphere as old acquaintances were renewed after a long and isolated winter. This would make the job of making maple syrup and sugar a very joyous occasion. The men would continue to hunt and the women and children would run the sugar camps.

A sugar boiling wigwam would be built in the same manner as the oblong wigwam described in the "Shelter" section above except the footprint of this wigwam would be about thirty feet long and sixteen feet wide. The fire pit would run the length of the structure and a hanging frame about 4 feet high would serve to hang the cooking kettles on. Copper kettles were used to boil the sap and the fires were tended continually. A smaller tepee type structure would also be erected to store the sugar making utensils in as well as wigwams for the families to live in.

When the wigwams were ready the trees were tapped with spiles. This is done by first cutting a groove into the tree on the sunny side about 3 feet above the roots. The spiles are then pounded into the tree to a depth of approximately 3 inches and sealed with hot pitch. The spiles were made from elderberry stems with the pith pushed out, one end sharpened, and the other end notched to hold the sap pail. The pails were made of birch bark and folded at the bottom, not sewn. A small pail could fill up in an hour at the height of the season. These were collected in the morning and at night.

Toboggans were used to haul the buckets of sap back to the boiling wigwam. The toboggans were made of hardwood cut during the winter when the trees have no sap. The front end was heated by boiling and bent upwards. They were pulled from the front but had a rope tied to the back so one person could control any sliding downhill.

The sap was poured into the copper kettles and continuously boiled until evaporation left sweet syrup. It takes thirty to forty gallons of sap to boil down to one gallon of syrup. With more boiling and evaporation the syrup would crystallize leaving a solid maple sugar product. This crystallized sugar was the bulk of their product but just before crystallization some of the very thick syrup would be poured into wooden moulds where it would harden to make a sort of rock candy. A fourth sugar product was made by pouring some of the thick syrup into the snow to cool it very quickly. In this case, the syrup would not crystallize but turn into a kind of taffy.[102] People would be assigned times to tend the fires and continually stir the kettles to prevent the sap from burning. This went on until the sap stopped running at which time the spiles were removed and the tree sealed with pitch. Utensils were stored in the storage tepee until next year and the group would move on to the fishing camps.

Since the hunting camps and the sugar bushes were far inland and too far to have carried their good canoes the Saugeen Ojibwa would build temporary ones from the bark of elm trees. These were made entirely out of one roll of the bark of the swamp-elm. It was a ruder canoe than the birch bark one described above as it was merely sewn up at both ends and the seams gummed. Two thwarts were then fastened to the upper edges of the canoe to keep it spread to a width of about 3½ feet. All of the produce from the hunt and the sugar camps were loaded into these temporary canoes and they were only used to descend the fast-moving rivers that flowed into Lake Huron. This also served to protect the good birch bark canoes as the white water rapids of the Saugeen and Maitland Rivers could easily damage them.[103]

---

102 Kohl, J.G., *Kitchi-Gami*, Chapman and Hall, London: 1860, 323-24.

103 Strickland, Major, C.M., *Twenty-seven Years in Canada West or The Experience of an Early Settler*, ed. Agnes Strickland, Volume II, Richard Bentley Publisher, London: 1853, 49-50.

CHAPTER 22

Fishing Camps

Many different kinds of fish were caught and in various ways. The rivers and streams provided brook trout, perch and bass. Lake Huron produced very large lake trout. Major Strickland was travelling on a schooner bound for Mackinaw in the early 1800's when met by nine canoes of Ojibwa fishermen who came on board to barter. One of the passengers traded for a lake trout weighing "no less than seventy-two pounds".[104] Herring was also taken from the lake, but the sturgeon was a particular delicacy. One of the main staples, of course, was whitefish. Whitefish was most plentiful and was so tasty it could be eaten quite regularly without becoming tiresome. Its meat was snow white and when boiled to perfection it became rather flaky but not dry. One of the favourite fishing areas for the Saugeen Ojibwa was the Fishing Islands, a number of small islands off the Lake Huron shoreline north of the Saugeen River.

The Ojibwa used various methods of fishing including spearing, netting, line and hook, and weirs. Spearing was extensively used. A pole 8 to 10 feet long and approximately 1½ inch in diameter at the butt end was used to make spears. The points were made from two pieces of ¼ inch iron rod twelve to fifteen inches long. A long point was filed on one end and a short end was filed the other end of each rod. One rod was about an inch longer than the other. The short points were bent at 90-degree angles about 3/8 of an inch long. A couple of barbs were cut in the rods with a cold chisel. The butt end of the spear was cut with a groove about six inches deep. The sharp ends of the rods would be forced

---

104 Ibid. 132-33.

into the groove with the barbs facing each other and the end of the spear wrapped with cord or rawhide. The prongs would be tapered slightly outward.

Spearing was done in summer and winter as well as both day and night. At night torches were used. Sturgeons were speared in the winter on the ice. A hole was cut in the ice about 2 feet in diameter. A small hut of poles and animal hide was built over this hole and the fisherman would crawl into the hut face down with his head over the hole but leave his legs outside. Daylight would light up the water beneath the transparent ice all around the hole and the artificial darkness produced by the hut and the fisherman's head prevented any reflection. The fisherman could see to a depth of forty feet watching for any fish swimming by. He could then thrust his spear at his unsuspecting prey.

Nets were used during the spring fish runs. Dip nets were fashioned by attaching a net about 2 feet long to a hoop and attaching the hoop to a long pole. Fishermen would then canoe out into the rapids at the mouth of the river. With one standing in the canoe while the other steered he would dip for white fish all the while keeping his balance. One swoop of the net would catch 7 or 8 fish at a time, which would be deposited into the bottom of the canoe in one motion. When the canoe was full they would be dumped on the shore and the fishermen would return to the rapids. Only the Ojibwa were known to fish in such a manner and with such a high degree of efficiency.

A lure was sometimes used when spearing the fish from an ice hole. It would be fashioned from a piece of wood or bone and sometimes dyed blue like a small herring. It would be tied to a line and weighted down with a piece of lead. Larger fish would then be enticed to the top of the water and when near enough to the opening would be speared.[105]

Fish weirs were also built during the spawning runs, which would force them into the holding pens for harvesting.

The following is a description of how fish were traditionally dried: Pat and Rebecca Shewaybick and translator Roy Spence from Webikwe, Ontario, visited the Bay Mills Indian Community Gnoozhekaaning Cultural Center June 21-22, 2000. Webikwe is a small northern Ontario community of about 600 Ahnishenahbek who still follow the old ways. The Shewaybicks and their children often spend weeks in the woods

---

105 Kohl, J.G. *Kitchi-Gami*, 325-31.

hunting and gathering. They visited Bay Mills, on the Lake Superior shoreline about 20 miles west of the Soo Locks, to show the community there how to powder fish so it can be preserved without refrigeration. Whitefish provided by a tribal fisher was used for the lesson.

The Shewaybick family also shared their traditional philosophy of life. According to Roy, it's up to them to look after each other and the land, and in this way, they can preserve their way of life. Roy, a Webikwe council member, works hard to educate the Ontario government leaders about the Ahnishenahbek culture.

First, a tepee is put up to smoke the fish. Juniper boughs are then gathered and placed in the tepee to keep the dampness out. The fish are then prepared for smoking. The heads and spines are removed, but both fillets remain attached to the tail. The bones keep the flesh from falling apart during smoking. The cleaned fish are then placed on drying sticks. The fish smoke with the sides held apart by the stick, to facilitate smoking. The smoked fish are pulled out of their skins and chunked into a heavy iron skillet to be powdered. The bones are kept in the mixture and fall apart much as canned salmon bones do, providing more nutrition. The fish is stirred back and forth over the heat, breaking it up more and more until it is completely dried and powdered, and ready to store.[106]

---

106 A description complete with photos of powdering fish using traditional native methods can be seen at http://www.great-lakes.net/teach/history/native/native_9.html accessed June 24, 2005.

CHAPTER 23

Conclusion

Both history and culture are important facets for a people to protect. One of the ways of doing this is through storytelling. This is important for the community to do, especially a community that is traditionally an oral one. Of course, storytelling can now be provided in written form in a variety of books and tracts.

One of the best ways of preserving a community's history and culture is by sharing it with others. For example, a heritage centre, with working elements, can be not only used by the community but can be aimed at the tourism industry as well. This form of sharing not only promotes goodwill between peoples but also provides a way for the facility to be viable by being at least partly self-sustaining. It is hoped that this report will be of some use in the planning stages of such an endeavour providing ideas and instilling pride in the things the Ojibwa of Saugeen Territory have both accomplished and endured.

Appendices

APPENDIX 1[107]

Agents and Missionary's Report 1858.

CHIPPEWAS OF SAUGEEN AND OWEN SOUND.

Captⁿ Anderson's Evidence. Appendix No. 29. Since the Report of the Commissioners of 1842, considerable changes have taken place among this Tribe.

Subsequently to the surrender made to Sir Francis Head in 1836, the Indians divided themselves into two Bands, one of which settled at the the mouth of the Saugeen River, while the other chose for its location a spot in the bight of the Bay of Sydenham. With the help of the Govern-

107 From Appendix 21 of the Appendix to the Sixteenth Volume of the Journals of the Legislative Assembly of the Province of Canada, 25th February to 16th August 1858.

ment, they erected a church, school house, and comfortable houses, at each of the Settlements.

In 1854 a cession of almost the entire Peninsula was obtained from them, reserves to the extent of 43,839 acres being only retained for their own occupation, of which 11,453 acres on the east were by mutual consent, considered to belong to the Band living at Newash or Owen's Sound. The Reserves at Saugeen and Chief's Point, on the west, containing about 10,300 acres, are for the benefit of the Saugeens ; that at Colpoy's Bay, for the Band of that name, containing about 6000 acres ; and that at Cape Croker, by admeasurement, 15,586 acres, is common to the Saugeen and Owen Sound Bands.

This arrangement made them distinct Bands, recognized as having separate and exclusive interests in the different Reserves on the two sides of the Peninsula. It will therefore be more clear to give, in separate sections, the information which we have been able to collect concerning them.

CHIPPEWAS AND POTTAWATAMIES OF SAUGEEN.

This Band resides on the tract retained for them near the town of Southampton. The Reserves appropriated to their own use are as follows :

1. A Block of land, bounded on the west by a straight line running due north from the River Saugeen where it is entered by a ravine immediately to the West of the Village ; on the south by the strip of land surrendered in 1851 ; on the east by a line drawn from a spot on the coast at a distance of about 9½ miles from the western boundary, and running parallel thereto till it meets the northern of the aforementioned surrendered strip. This Reserve contains about 8600 acres, and is excellent land.

2. That tract of land called Chief's Point ; bounded on the east by a line drawn from a spot half a mile up the Sable River, and continued in a northerly direction to the Bay ; and upon all other sides by the Bay. .

3. The cluster of Islands lying to the north of Chief's Point, and known as the "Fishing Islands." They are 13 in number, and are principally valuable as a fishing station. The autumn catch of fish is usually very large, as the fish are found in great numbers off this part of the coast. The Islands are now leased to a white man at an annual rental of £75 cy.

In spite of the advantages enjoyed by these Indians, but little can be said for their improvement. It appears that in 1837 they numbered about 197 including 20 Pottawatamies, and were, in the opinion of the Chief Superintendent, very poor and miserable, trusting very much to hunting and fishing for their support. The same may be said of them still. They share in the largest annuity of any Tribe in Canada, and are now entitled to large sums arising from the sale of their land and the rental of their fisheries. Their Reserve near Southampton is the richest part of the whole Peninsula, capable of raising excellent crops of corn and other produce. During the period of twelve years that they have occupied this tract, they have had repeated supplies of farming implements, cattle and grain, but such is their indolence and improvidence that they had in part to be supported during the last winter by the Department.

Their Superintendent, Captain Anderson, says, in August last, of them: "Three yoke of oxen, which they paid a high price for last year, "were so ill cared for during the winter that they are now barely able to "walk about to nip the sprouting grass, and they have a white man with "his team actually employed at $4 a-day to plough up their little gardens, "while groups of hearty-looking men of their own Tribe are laughing and "smoking time away without a thought for the future.

"To shew the improvidence of these poor creatures, a merchant at "Saugeen (Mr. Jardine) informs me that he for his share bought from them "last autumn 300 barrels of fish, and other parties got at least 500 more "making 1000 barrels, for which was paid $3 per barrel. Notwithstanding "this favourable opportunity to do so, they did not reserve a supply for "their families during the winter, and had not the Department supplied "them with provisions, it is said some of them must have perished. This "spring they made a large quantity of sugar which they sold at five pence "per lb., and still they appear to be largely in debt. It is right however Revd Mr. Kibbage's "to say that a more favourable opinion of them is ex-
Evidence.   "pressed by their Missionary."

Their present numbers are 256. The increase since 1844 may be partly due to immigration, as during the last year the deaths have preponderated over the births.

The principal causes of death are stated to be intemperance, exposure, insufficiency of wholesome food and pulmonary complaints.

They have a resident Missionary of the Wesleyan persuasion among them, and the school is kept by his son. The attendance however is very irregular, never exceeding 20. The average, when all the families are in the village, is stated to be about 10, but sometimes the school is closed for three or four weeks together owing to the absence of the children.

The band possess as public property a frame church, a school-house and three yoke of oxen. Their village, which is beautifully situated on the high ground, on the right bank of the river, contains 16 frame and 14 log houses; They cultivate 294½ acres, which are not held in common, but divided into separate little farms. On these however they only raised in 1856:

	Bushels.
Wheat,	81
Indian Corn,	137½
Pease,	11
Potatoes,	1213

The greatest quantity of land under cultivation belonging to an individual Indian, amounts to 14 acres.

The present revenue of the band is $5382 50 derived from the following sources:

Share of annuity..........................	$2,500
Interest on land Sales......................	2,712 50
Rent of Fishing Islands.................	150
	$5382 50

The interest on the proceeds of the land sales will of course be largely increased when the whole of the peninsula is sold, and the receipts invested for their benefit.

CHIPPEWAS OF NEWASH OR OWEN'S SOUND.

By the surrender of 1854, there were reserved for this Band, a tract on the Western side of Owen's Sound, stretching ten miles along the shore, and extending two miles into the interior of the Peninsula. On this were situated their villages.

A considerable quantity of land was also retained at Cape Croker, a long point separating Melville Sound and Colpoy's Bay on the western side of the Georgian Bay, for the use of the two Bands.

The Islands on the western coast of the last mentioned bay, are also unsurrendered. The principal are White Cloud Island, Griffith's Island and Hay Island. They are described as of some extent, (estimated at about 15,000 acres) containing good land and covered with an excellent growth of hardwood.

This Band have lately surrendered the location on the shores of Owen's Sound from which they derive their appellation. It has been sold for their benefit, and they are in progress of being settled on the reserve at Cape Croker.

The extent of this tract is 15,586 acres, laid out into farms of twenty-five acres. This arrangement will eventually make, it is hoped, on this spot a settlement round which may be concentrated all the Indians now inhabiting the Saugeen Peninsula.

One of the farms will be appropriated to each Indian family, as at present constituted. Young men who will in the year 1860 have attained the age of 21 years, are also entitled to receive lots. They will also receive perpetual licenses of occupation for their lots, by which means it is hoped to increase their interest in the improvement of the land and stimulate their industry. Such of the Tribe as are now living in houses formerly built by the Indian Department for them, will have houses given to them, and will receive the value of their improvements on the land they now relinquish together with $40 apiece as a sum to help them in clearing and stocking their new farms. The Band is also entitled to a further amount sufficient to build a Church and such other permanent improvement as may be approved by the Governor General.

The Funds to meet these stipulations are to be taken from the proceeds of the land sold. This is the first experiment combining small compact farms, written promises of undisturbed possession of their lots by each family, and the outlay of part of the principal of the land sales for the improvement of the new home of the Indians.

The site chosen for their village is a gentle slope on the shores of a sheltered cove called McGregor's Bay. The land is a deep vegetable mould easily worked, while in the vicinity of the village the land is described to be " of very good quality, free from surface stone, and well " timbered,"......" the land would be easily cleared, there being but " little underbrush, and the woods clear and open."

The fisheries, though not equal to those on the western side of the Peninsula, are considerable, and will constitute no inconsiderable part of the means of subsistence available for the Band.

The description given of the Saugeen branch of this Tribe may be considered as in great measure applying to these Indians also. Considered as a whole they are squalid, thriftless and much addicted to intemperance.

There are however some gratifying exceptions, and a series of resolutions have this year been voluntarily signed by the chiefs and a large part of the band, agreeing to relinquish the use of all intoxicating beverages, on penalty of forfeiting all participation in the moneys receivable by the Tribe.

The same punishment has been attached to breaches of the matrimonial law. This movement has been entirely spontaneous and is beginning to be acted upon.

The numbers of this Band are 238. The births and deaths during the year 1856, as given by their Missionary, were respectively 9 and 33. The Band is however recruited from time to time by stray members of different Tribes; while considered therefore as Chippewas, they reckon among their strength a few Pottawatamies, Ottawas and Iroquois. There are too some individuals adopted from other tribes. The Iroquois who are found here, are some families who have intermarried with the Pottawatamies, and are now incorporated with the Chippewas. They originally formed a portion of a party who came from the Sault St. Louis in Lower Canada, whence they were induced to emigrate some years ago, in consequence of difficulties arising there, and were located in the Saugeen territory by the Earl of Elgin. Finding themselves however from their position there deprived of the services of a Clergyman of their own persuasion, and from other causes, the majority of them returned last year to Caughnawaga and St. Regis, leaving a few of their number as above stated.

There are also 29 individuals who have removed hither from the Manitoulin Islands. The last census gives an increase since last year in the aggregate of the bands resident here and at Saugeen, of 8 persons, but it does not specify where the augmentation has taken place.

The Newash Indians are principally Wesleyans, there are however many members of the Church of England, and some Roman Catholics.

They have a resident Wesleyan Missionary, and two Schools, one kept by a brother of the Clergyman; the average number of scholars at this School is about ten, but the attendance is very irregular, and frequently no school is held for weeks; the other School is taught by the native Interpreter, who was educated at the Upper Canada College, and whose attainments are far above those of most Indians. The usual number of children at this School is 12, but like most of the small Indian Schools, the result is most unsatisfactory as will be seen by the number of children who never go to School. The number returned by the local Superintendent as of an age to go there is 50, while the aggregate of those on the list at the two Schools is only 22. The attendance of those on the

School rolls is so inconstant that they make but little improvement, either in the rudiments of knowledge imparted to them, or in any other desirable acquirement.

All scholastic education is likely to be interrupted for a short time owing to the removal of the band, and the statistical returns given below must be understood as applying only to the Village which is in course of abandonment.

They own as public property a frame church and a mission house, two log school houses, and one frame barn. They also possess four ploughs, three yoke of oxen, and one fanning mill. These last have been taken so little care of, as to be of little use, but the following statement of the crops raised last year will shew how little value they attach to agricultural improvement.

Out of 1,980½ acres in the possession of individuals, only 273½ have been cleared, and of these but 251½ were under crop.

On these they raised—

	Bushels.
Wheat	49
Indian Corn	122
Pease	38
Oats	2
Potatoes	935

and 8½ tons of Hay.

There are belonging to different members of the band (besides those held in common) four yoke of oxen, four cows and five heads of young stock.

In these returns are included the dwelling houses, barns, &c., live stock and crops owned by the Locquoit.   They also hold twenty-seven frame and eight log houses, besides seven log barns. The revenues of this band are derived from their share of the annuity belonging to the Chippewas of Saugeen, amounting to £625 or $2,500.

They also participate in the land sales of the Peninsula as surrendered in 1854, amounting at present to $2,712 50, the funds accruing from the township of Sarawak, and the town plot of Brooke will belong exclusively to them. They already derive $4,140 46 from this source. This Band has also a share in the rent of the "Fishing Island" amounting to $150 per annum.

Chippewas of Shawanega and Sandy Island.   This Band derive their name from an Island about 50 miles north-west from Penetanguishene, where they pass part of the year spending the rest of their time on the main land. They support themselves principally by the Chase and by fishing. Their attempts at farming are of the rudest description, their implements being only a few axes and iron hoes; or in the absence of the latter, crooked sticks are used to scratch up the Earth. Their small patches of Indian Corn and Potatoes are looked upon rather as a means of supplying luxuries, than as able to afford the staple of their subsistence during the winter.

They were originally under Captain Ironside's superintendence, and came from near the Sault St. Marie in 1850, when they numbered 93. The census of this year shews a total of 145, but Captain Anderson re-

much that is probably due to the additions made to the Band by individuals migrating from other quarters. They are all Heathens, having resisted all attempts to civilize or christianize them.

Their Annual income is $303.20 derived from their share of the money voted by the Provincial Legislature to the Indians of Lakes Huron and Superior.

APPENDIX 2[108]

Letter by Sir Francis Bond Head

108 Head, Sir Francis Bond. *Communications and Despatches Relating to Recent Negotiations with the Indians*, Printed at the Office of the British Colonies, 1-2.

It appears that these Islands in which we are now assembled in Council, are, as well as all those on the north shore of Lake Huron, alike claimed by the English, the Ottawas and the Chippewas.

I consider that from their facilities, and from their being surrounded by innumerable fishing Islands, they might be made a most desirable place of residence for many Indians who wish to be civilized as well as to be totally separated from the Whites, and I now tell you that your Great Father will withdraw his claim to these Islands, and allow them to be applied for that purpose.

. Are you, therefore, the Ottawas and Chippewas, willing to relinquish your respective claims to these Islands, and make them the property (under your Great Father's control) of all Indians whom he shall allow to reside on them? If so, affix your marks to this proposal.

(Signed)   F. B. HEAD.

MANATOWANING, August 9, 1836.

Signed by all the CHIEFS.

The surrender of the Saugin Territory has long been a desideratum in the Province, and it is now especially important, as it will appear to be the first fruits of the political tranquility which has been attained.

I feel confident that the Indians, when settled by us in the manner I have detailed, will be better off than they were—that the position they occupy can bona fide be fortified against the encroachments of the whites—while, on the other hand, there can be no doubt that the acquisition of their vast and fertile territory will be hailed with joy by the whole Province.

I have, &c.,

The Right Honorable   (Signed)   F. B. HEAD.
    The Lord Glenelg.

A true copy, J. Joseph.

(Copy.)

MY CHILDREN:—

Seventy snow seasons have now passed away since we met in Council at the crooked place, (Niagara) at which time and place your great Father, the King and the Indians of North America, tied their hands together by the wampum of friendship.

Since that period various circumstances have occurred to separate from your great Father many of his red children, and as an unavoidable increase of white population, as well as the progress of civilization, have had the natural effect of impoverishing your hunting grounds, it has become necessary that new arrangements should be entered into for the purpose of protecting you from the encroachments of the whites.

In all parts of the world, farmers seek for uncultivated land as eagerly as you, my red children, hunt in your great forests for game. If you would cultivate your land, it would then be considered your own property ; in the same way as your dogs are considered among yourselves to belong to those who have reared them ; but uncultivated land is like wild animals, and your Great Father who has hitherto protected you, has now great difficulty in securing it for you from the whites who are hunting to cultivate it.

Under these circumstances, I have been obliged to consider what is best to be done for the Red Children of the Forest, and I now tell you my thoughts.

It appears that these Islands in which we are now assembled in Council, are, as well as all those on the north shore of Lake Huron, alike claimed by the English, the Ottawas and the Chippewas.

I consider that from their facilities, and from their being surrounded by innumerable fishing Islands, they might be made a most desirable place of residence for many Indians who wish to be civilized as well as to be totally separated from the Whites, and I now tell you that your Great Father will withdraw his claim to these Islands, and allow them to be applied for that purpose.

Are you, therefore, the Ottawas and Chippewas, willing to relinquish your respective claims to these Islands, and make them the property (under your Great Father's control) of all Indians whom he shall allow to reside on them ? If so, affix your marks to this proposal.

MANATOWANING, August 9, 1836.   (Signed)   F. B. HEAD.

                                                   Signed by all the CHIEFS.

TO THE SAUKINS.

MY CHILDREN:—

You have heard the proposal I have just made to the Chippewas and Ottawas, by which it has been agreed between them and your Great Father, that these Islands (Manitoulin) on which we are now assembled in Council, should be made the property, (under your Great Father's control,) of all Indians whom he shall allow to reside on them.

I now propose to you that you should surrender to your Great Father, the Saukin Territory you at present occupy, and that you shall repair either to this Island or to that part of your Territory, which lies in the north of Owen's Sound ; upon which proper houses shall be built for you, and proper assistance given, to enable you to become civilized and to cultivate land ; which your Great Father engages forever to protect for you from the encroachments of the Whites.

Are you, therefore, the Saukin Indians, willing to accede to this arrangement ? If so, affix your marks to this my proposal.

MANATOWANNING, August 9, 1836.   (Signed)   F. B. HEAD.

                                                   Signed by all the CHIEFS.

Treaties 45, 45 ½, & 72[109]

MY CHILDREN:

Seventy snow seasons have now passed away since we met in Council at the crooked place (Niagara), at which time and place your Great Father, the King, and the Indians of North America tied their hands together by the wampum of friendship.

Since that period various circumstances have occurred to separate from your Great Father many of his red children, and as an unavoidable increase of white population, as well as the progress of cultivation, have had the natural effect of impoverishing your hunting grounds it has become necessary that new arrangements should be entered into for the purpose of protecting you from the encroachments of the whites.

In all parts of the world farmers seek for uncultivated land as eagerly as you, my red children, hunt in your forest for game. If you would cultivate your land it would then be considered your own property, in the same way as your dogs are considered among yourselves to belong to those who have reared them; but uncultivated land is like wild animals, and your Great Father, who has hitherto protected you, has now great difficulty in securing it for you from the whites, who are hunting to cultivate it.

Under these circumstances, I have been obliged to consider what is best to be done for the red children of the forest, and I now tell you my thoughts.

It appears that these islands on which we are now assembled in Council are, as well as all those on the north shore of Lake Huron, alike claimed by the English, the Ottawas and the Chippewas.

I consider that from their facilities and from their being surrounded by innumerable fishing islands, they might be made a most desirable place of residence for many Indians who wish to be civilized, as well as to be totally separated from the whites; and I now tell you that your Great Father will withdraw his claim to these islands and allow them to be applied for that purpose.

Are you, therefore, the Ottawas and Chippewas, willing to relinquish your respective claims to these islands and make them the property (under your Great Father's control) of all Indians whom he shall allow to reside on them; if so, affix your marks to this my proposal.

MANITOWANING, 9th August, 1836.

F. B. HEAD,
J. B. ASSEKINACK,
MOKOMMUNISH, (totem)
TAWACKKUCK, .
KIMEWEN (totem),
KITCHEMOKOMON (totem),
PESCIATAWICK (totem),
PAIMAUSEGAI (totem),
NAINAWMUTTEBE (totem),
MOSUNEKO (totem),
KEWUCKANCE (totem),
SHAWENAUSEWAY (totem),
ESPANIOLE (totem),
SNAKE (totem),
PAUTUNSEWAY (totem),
PAIMAUQUMESTCAM (totem),
WAGEMAUQUIN (totem).

No. 45½.

To the Saukings:

MY CHILDREN,

You have heard the proposal I have just made to the Chippewas and Ottawas, by which it has been agreed between them and your Great Father that these islands (Manatoulin), on which we are now assembled, should be made, in Council, the property (under your Great Father's control) of all Indians whom he shall allow to reside on them.

I now propose to you that you should surrender to your Great Father the Sauking Territory you at present occupy, and that you should repair either to this island or to that part of your territory which lies on the north of Owen Sound, upon which proper houses shall be built for you and proper assistance given to enable you to become civilized and to cultivate land, which your Great Father engages for ever to protect for you from the encroachments of the whites.

Are you therefore, the Sauking Indians, willing to accede to this arrangement; if so, affix your marks to this my proposal.

MANITOWANING, 9th August. 1836.

Witness:

T. G. ANDERSON, *S.I.A.*,
JOSEPH STINSON, *Genl. Supt. of Wes-layan Missions,*
ADAM ELLIOT,
JAMES EVANS,
F. L. INGALL, *Lieut. 15th Regt. Com-mandg. Detacht.,*
TALFOURD W. FIELD, *Dist. Agent.*

F. B. HEAD,
METIEWABE (totem),
ALEXANDER (totem) KAQUTA BUNE-VAIKRAR,
KOWGISAWIS (totem),
METTAWANSH (totem),

CROWN LAND DEPARTMENT,
TORONTO, 20th February, 1857.
Entered upon the records of this Department on L. W. No. 39.

No. 72.

SURRENDER OF THE SAUGEEN PENINSULA.

We, the Chiefs, Sachems and Principal Men of the Indian Tribes resident at Saugeen, Owen Sound, confiding in the wisdom and protecting care of our Great Mother across the Big Lake, and believing that our Good Father, His Excellency the Earl of Elgin and Kincardine, Governor General of Canada, is anxiously desirous to promote those interests which will most largely conduce to the welfare of His red children, have now, being in full Council assembled, in presence of the Superintendent General of Indian Affairs, and of the young men of both tribes, agreed that it will be highly desirable for us to make a full and complete surrender unto the Crown of that Peninsula known as the Saugéen and Owen Sound Indian Reserve, subject to certain restrictions and reservations to be hereinafter set forth. We have therefore set our marks to this document, after having heard the same read to us, and do hereby surrender the whole of the above named tract of country, bounded on the south by a straight line drawn from the Indian village of Saugeen to the Indian village of Nawash, in continuation of the northern limits of the narrow strip recently surrendered by us to the Crown; and bounded on the north-east and west by Georgian Bay and Lake Huron, with the following reservations, to wit: 1st. For the benefit of the Saugeen Indians we reserve all that block of land bounded on the west by a straight line running due north from the River Saugeen, at the spot where it is

by a straight line running due north from the River Saugeen, at the spot where it is entered by a ravine, immediately to the west of the village, and over which a bridge has recently been constructed, to the shore of Lake Huron; on the south by the aforesaid northern limit of the lately surrendered strip; on the east by a line drawn from a spot upon the coast at a distance of about (9½) nine miles and a half from the western boundary aforesaid, and running parallel thereto until it touches the aforementioned northern limits of the recently surrendered strip; and we wish it to be clearly understood that we wish the Peninsula at the mouth of the Saugeen River to the west of the western boundary aforesaid to be laid out in townpark lots and sold for our benefit without delay; and we also wish it to be understood that our surrender includes that parcel of land which is in continuation of the strip recently surrendered to the Saugeen River

We do also reserve to ourselves that tract of land called Chief's Point, bounded on the east by a line drawn from a spot half a mile up the Sable River, and continued in a northerly direction to the bay, and upon all other sides by the lake.

2nd. We reserve for the benefit of the Owen Sound Indians all that tract bounded on the south by the northern limit of the continuation of the strip recently surrendered; on the north-west by a line drawn from the north easterly angle of the aforesaid strip (as it was surrendered in 1851, in a north easterly direction); on the south-east by the sound extending to the southern limit of the Caughnawaga Settlement; on the north by a line two miles in length and forming the said southern limit. And we also reserve to ourselves all that tract of land called Cape Crocker, bounded on three sides by Georgian Bay, on the south-west side by a line drawn from the bottom of Nochemowenaing Bay to the mouth of Sucker River, and we include in the aforesaid surrender the parcel of land contained in the continuation to Owen's Sound of the recently surrendered strip aforesaid.

3rd. We do reserve for the benefit of the Colpoy's Bay Indians, in the presence and with the concurrence of John Beattie, who represents the tribe at this Council, a block of land containing 6,000 acres, and including their village, and bounded on the north by Colpoy's Bay.

13½*

196

All which reserves we hereby retain to ourselves and our children in perpetuity, and it is agreed that the interest of the principal sum arising out of the sale of our lands be regularly paid to them so long as there are Indians left to represent our tribe without diminution at half yearly periods.

And we hereby request the sanction of our Great Father the Governor General to this surrender, which we consider highly conducive to our general interests.

Done in Council, at Saugeen, this thirteenth day of October, 1854.

It is understood that no islands are included in this surrender.

Signed and sealed:
L. OLIPHANT,
    Supt. Genl. Indian Affairs.

PETER JACOBS,
    Missionary.

Witnesses:
  JAS. ROSS, M.P.P.,
  C. RANKIN, P.L.S.,
  A. McNABB,
    Crown Land Agent.

JOHN (totem) KADCHOBKWUN,	[L.S.]
ALEX. (totem) MADWAYOSH,	[L.S.]
JOHN (totem) MANEDSWAB,	[L.S.]
JNO. THOS. (totem) WAHBUNDICK,	[L.S.]
PETER (totem) JONES,	[L.S.]
DAVID SAWYER,	[L.S.]
JOHN H. BEATT.	[L.S.]
THOMAS (totem) PABAHMOSH,	[L.S.]
JOHN (totem) MADWASHEMIND,	[L.S.]
JOHN (totem) JOHNSTON,	[L.S.]
JOHN AUNIEOAHBOWH,	[L.S.]
JAMES NEWASH,	[L.S.]
THOMAS (totem) WAHBUHDICK,	[L.S.]
CHARLES KEESHICK.	[L.S.]

APPENDIX 3[110]

Land Surveyor's Report to Indian Agent Anderson

Sub-enclosure 3, to Enclosure in No. 1.

Sir, 2 August 1854.

By a rough estimate there appears to be in the whole of the Indian tract to the north of Derby and Arran, about 450,000 acres.

Of this 450,000 acres, about 190,000 lies to the south of a line from the middle of the group of Fishing Islands to Colpoy's Bay, and about 260,000 to the north of that line, terminating at Cabot's Head and Cape Hind; this latter part probably contains but little that can be cultivated, being believed to be very rocky.

Of the 190,000 acres 130,000 is included within the two parcels desired to be retained by the Indians, including all the coast, both of Georgian Bay and Lake Huron, as far north as Colpoy's Bay and the Fishing Islands, leaving about 60,000 acres south of these two mentioned points, while they are willing to part with this 60,000 acres being included, and in a wedge-like shape.

Should they persist in objecting to sell any other portion of the 190,000 acres than this inland wedge-like piece, it is obvious that the principal advantage aimed at, both for themselves and the whites, will in a great measure fail, since the portions they thus propose to retain (although with no idea of using them), are the parts most desired by the whites for the formation of settlements, and for which, consequently, they would be most willing to pay large prices.

Such particularly are the parts including the mill site on the Au Sable River, the coast opposite the Fishing Islands, where a town may be laid out to advantage.

These are the parts which the sale of them being managed for the Indians as white men would manage them for himself, would produce them a very large sum and very speedily. The part they offer to surrender will neither sell so readily nor realize anything like as large a price; and in the mean time, as long as they retain the other more desirable parts, there is no doubt they will constantly be assailed as they have hitherto been by companies of speculators desirous of purchasing from them, &c., and to one or two of whom they have already shown a disposition to yield, although it is evident it would be greatly to their disadvantage to do so.

I hope, therefore both for the Indian's sake, and to allow the white settlements a chance to extend, you will recommend the more limited reservations.

I am, &c.

Captain Anderson, S.I.A. (signed) C. Rankin.

---

110 Indian Department of Canada, Return to an Address of the Honourable The House of Commons, dated 28 April 1856, Viscount Goderich, 1856 13.

APPENDIX 4

Maps

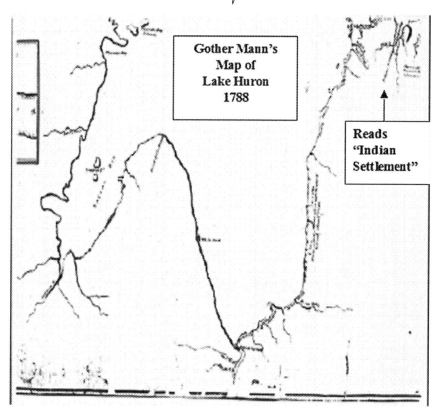

Gother Mann's
Map of
Lake Huron
1788

Reads
"Indian
Settlement"

Sketch of Lake Huron, 1788 circumnavigated by Gother Mann,
Capt. commanding Royal Engineers in Canada.[111]

111 Library and Archives Canada/Maps, Plans and Charts/n0018558k

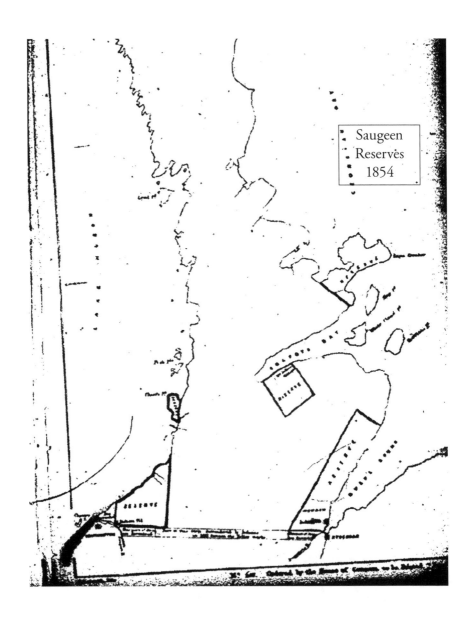

Saugeen
Reservès
1854

112 Indian Department of Canada, Return to an Address of the Honourable The
House of Commons, dated 28 April 1856, Viscount Goderich, 1856

APPENDIX 5[113]

Midéwiwin Ceremony

Having been informed that the Indians were about to attend a Medai Kechewegoondewin, or Conjurers great feast, I determined if practicable, to witness the ceremony: first, for my own satisfaction; and secondly, with the view of furnishing the readers of the Guardian with the particulars.

This feast was given, and the ceremony attended to, in order to initiate two Indian children into the order of Medai or Conjurors, or as some writers on Indian customs have been pleased to designate this class of men, the "priesthood". The ground selected for this occasion, was a sandy spot on the bank of the St. Clair River, about half a mile distant from the Mission house, close by the graves of the sleeping fathers of this once numerous tribe; a spot for which the Indians generally have a great veneration.

Early in the morning of the day appointed, the women assembled, with implements suitable for their labour, and levelled the ground, carefully removing all the small stumps and roots, and making the same perfectly smooth. Small stakes, at regular distances, were driven into the ground, enclosing a plot of about fifty feet in length and 25 in breadth, to these at the height of about 5 feet were tied with bark, long poles, to which were hung canoe-sails, tent cloths, blankets, etc.; thus enclosing the whole, and excluding observations and entrance, except at each end where an opening of about 6 feet was left. In the centre were driven two strong stakes about two feet apart, to each of which was tied a wooden

---

113 Evans, J. *Christian* Guardian, January 28, 1835:45, reprinted in Graham, Elizabeth. *Medicine Man to Missionary*, Appendix II, 98-104.

image resembling the human figure, the head being loose in order to admit the body which was below, to be filled, as it was on this occasion, with kahskeken or medicine prepared from roots, barks, leaves, etc.

About noon, nine kettles, holding from two to four pails full, were placed before the company; some few were served from the same in tin pans but the greater part, unceremoniously, and in no small quantities, helped themselves. And the pork, hams, venison, ducks, squirrels, raccoons, bears meat and other game being boiled to shreds they found no difficulty in dispensing with forks, and in many cases with knives also, pulling the food to pieces, and appearing to comprehend the old proverb, "fingers were made before forks:" nor were they less forgetful of the Indian maxim "eat all that is set before you:" for it can scarcely be said the kettles were successively emptied, – but rather simultaneously; the company amounted to between one hundred and fifty and two hundred. This evidently gratifying part of the ceremony being ended, a select party consisting of the Medai or Conjurors, retired to the woods and spent nearly an hour in singing to the spirits; while the women fetched some straw and spread it around the enclosure, and made some other necessary arrangements. As the evening shadows closed in, the fires were lighted, one at each entrance, and the company began to take their seats. After some time, for Indian movements are generally very deliberately performed, all were seated, and one of the Medai took the Tatewaegun or drum and commenced slowly beating it at intervals of nearly a second, as a signal that all was now in readiness; upon which the men, women and children arose, and took their places in rows or rank within the enclosure; this done, the Medai began to beat more lively, two women accompanying the sound of the drum with the sheshegwun or rattle, while they struck a song and all began to dance; this consisted in a gentle and not ungraceful movement of the body, and occasionally a step or two with the feet. So regular and uniform is the movement and so grotesque the appearance, each being wrapped in a new white blanket, on which being a beautiful clear night, the moon, which was full, cast her silver light and gave a striking effect to the scene, that an observer can scarcely believe but that the ground on which he stands is in motion, and almost imagine himself to be moving in unison with the company. There were present nine male and two female Medin, the drum was alternately beat and the singing led by each about half an hour, while all joined in the chorus; the men occasionally singing softly, unaccompanied by the females, and at other times having pleasant voices, they produce, unasscociated with the recollection of paganism, not unpleasing music. This was the introduction to the ceremony of initiation. A little boy about six and a little girl about seven years of age were the subjects; these, who had accompanied the Medai to the words, now joined in the singing, and took a prominent place in the dance. After this dance, the drum having been beat by each Medai, all took their seats, and each took a dram of whiskey...

A blanket was now spread in the centre, and the two children were seated thereon, with their faces towards the images before mentioned; and pieces of blue and red cloth, containing about a quarter of a yard each were spread at their feet. Two women took their places behind them, in the parts they would be required to act in the ceremony. The oldest man in the tribe arose and spoke about fifteen minutes, addressing himself first to the men, then to the women and lastly to the children. Exhorting them to hold facts on the religion of their fathers; to be patient in enduring hardships; and urging on the children to observe mahgahtawin or blacking and fasting; (a religious ceremony) and closed by promising them, should they observe what he said, beards as white as his, which was silvered over with age and limbs as strong therewith; he then began a song in praise of the children seated in the centre, the chorus, in which all joined being: "Oh, Oh nejahnesun, ne nejahnesun" which ended all at once arose, crying "Wah wah wah" and commenced dancing and moving around the enclosure in file, keeping in their movements the most regular order, and timing their steps to the drums, rattles and vocal sounds. This exercise, which appeared to be a compliment to the children, all the song being in their praise, continued about fifteen or twenty minutes, and again all resumed their seats.

The Medai now arose, all the rest remaining seated in silence, and each took his or her kahshkekeh mahahkemoot, or medicine pouch, being an otter skin, containing from fifty to a hundred very small parcels of mahshkekeh, or medicine used in conjuring, consisting of roots, leaves, bark, cinnamon cloves, tobacco, a small wooden box, some mekis, or sea shells, a wooden snake, some porcupine quills, a mink or squirrel skin, also full of medicine, atahpejegun, or cord to tie prisoners in war, a sheshegwun, or rattle used in curing the sick; and a variety of other small articles – and hung it in the belt around the waist. The chief Medai taking the lead, the others following, walked slowly and majestically around the enclosure several times, the chief Medai pressing on them to attend to their duty on this occasion; after which each took his pouch from the belt in which it hung, and singing, kept the head of the skin moving up and down, thus beating time to their song. In a few minutes, continuing singing, they moved in file dancing towards the two children, carrying their skins in both hands, and giving them a gently undulating movement, similar to that of a snake in motion; each as he arrived presented the head of the skin to one and then to the other of the children's breasts, crying, "Hahwah yahwah." And at each presentation the women threw the children on their faces, raising them again for the next until the last, when the children were both left on their faces as if dead. All now uttered as loudly as possible, "Wah wah wah and quickly retreated in haste, as if afraid, to the end of the enclosure; the women, at the same time stooping down and applying their mouths to the ears of the children, called aloud, "Ahwah ahwah ahwah" repeating these sounds five times; and pointing north, east, south and west, and lastly into the ground, again cried, "Wah wah wah" and raised the children to a sitting posture. The Medai during this time continued singing and walking slowly around the enclosure until they arrived again opposite the children, where they all stood still with their mouths open, and the chief Medai took from his pouch a root, and breaking it into small pieces put into each Medai's mouth a piece, which was chewed as they danced around. On arriving at the children they successively spat a little of the juice on the breast, on each side the neck, and on the back of each of the children; walking around once more, they each took up the pieces of cloth which laid by the children, and muttered some words too low to be distinguished, and retired to the end of the ground. Here they commenced singing and taking their skins, gave them the undulating motion before mentioned; then they proceeded to the children from whom they retreated in haste, and fell one over the other at the entrance of the enclosure. In a little time they arose, placed themselves in a row, and looking directly upwards, their heads being thrown back as far as possible, each holding in his finger and thumb a small piece of mahskekeh, he put it five times into his own mouth, at each time crying "Yahahwah, Yahahwah, Yahahwah" and pointing to the four points and into the ground as before mentioned, they ran and fell at the other end of the encampment.

Each Medai now arose and made a speech, declaring the children to be regularly received into their community and to be constituted Medai, and that they should in future have the privilege of joining in every Medaiwegoontewin, and enjoining on each other to embrace every opportunity of instructing them in the wisdom of the Medai and promising them if these children endeavour to become wise, and attend to mahkahtiwin, (blacking and fasting) they would always own them as brethren among the Medai. The children were now led around the ground by their attendant women, and their right hands presented to every one present, the women shewing to everyone a small sea shell; after which all joined in singing and dancing...

J. EVANS, St. Clair Rapids 18th Dec. 1834

APPENDIX 6

Clan Systems

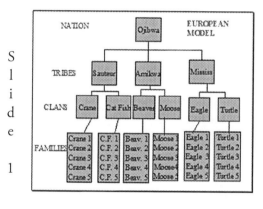

In the European model the nation is central and is made up of tribes. Tribes are made up of clans, which consist of families of both near and distant relatives. This makes families the lowest unit in the hierarchy.

In the First Nations Model the family totem is central. Each member was considered a near relative: there were no distant relatives. Bands were determined according to hunting territory. Any given family (totem) was scattered throughout the various bands. Language determined the nation and held it together. .

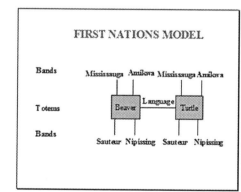

APPENDIX 7

Saugeen Ojibwa Names

Names from Curnoe

Ah-yah-bance was chief of the Saugeen Ojibwas in 1842...Racoon =
e: ssipan (Piggott and Grafstein)[114]

Kegedoons / Keketoonce [fl. 1829; disappeared and found dead near
Goderich in the fall of 1831], Ojibwa chief of the Naguhweseebe [Ausable
River / Port Franks] community, father of Thomas Bigcanoe; he camped
near Manestung [Goderich] in 1829; he met Kahkewaquonaby [Peter Jones]
on July 27, 1829 while canoeing south on Lake Huron; Jones described
him as an old chief and an associate of Chief Wawanosh; Keketoonce
told Jones that he would accept Christianity if Chief Wawanosh did
and vice versa; he also told Jones that he wished to settle at the Saugeen
River and to receive presents at the mouth of the Red River [Goderich] in
1829; Kegedoons travelled to the Credit River in December 1829 and was
converted to Christianity by the spring of 1831 (Kahkewaquonaby 1860:
239-240, 268; Smith 1987: 110-111). 'Brothers and Sisters, the Great Spirit
has planted a tree at this place whose top reaches the skies - you have found
this tree and are climbing up towards the abode of the Great Spirit' —Credit
River, December 1829[115] "The loss of Chief Kegedoons also proved a great
blow. The leader of the Saugeen Indians had welcomed Peter Jones during

---

114 Curnoe, *Deeds/Nations*, 33.

115 Ibid, 48.

Peter's visit to Lake Huron in late July 1829. That December Kegedoons and twenty of his people had travelled overland to the Credit to see for themselves the Christian settlement. Greatly impressed by what he found, Kegedoons rose at a prayer meeting and told his hosts: 'My brothers and sisters whilst in my own country I heard what the Great Spirit had done for you, so I came to see for myself what all this meant. I have opened my ears to the words spoken by your ministers & what I had heard by the hearing of the ear I now see with mine own eyes. Brothers & Sisters, the Great Spirit has planted a tree at this place whose top reaches the skies-you have found this tree and are climbing up towards the abode of the Great Spirit.' Most of the Saugeens in Kegedoons group converted to Christianity at the Credit. By the spring of 1831 nearly half of the two hundred Saugeens, including Kegedoons himself, had joined the Methodists. But that fall the chief disappeared. Near the new settlement of Goderich the Indians found his lifeless body, 'bruised and mangled in such a way as to make it evident that he had been murdered.' In Chief John Assance's words, 'we do not believe the whites would do this but fear some unknown people of our own colour-lurk about to shed our blood.' A century later Kegedoon's great-grandson still believed he had been murdered."[116]

Nawash / Naiwash / Naiwasha / Neywash [fl. 1813-1819], Odawa Nation, Saugeen community, war chief; he fought with Tecumseh at McGregor's Creek, October 3, 1813, and at the Battle of Moraviantown [Fairfield], October 5, 1813; Naiwash visited Québec City, February 14, 1814; Nawash attended and spoke at a conference at Burlington, June 14, 1814; made the rank of captain; Naiwash gave a speech about the loss of Tecumseh on October 6, 1814; Neywash settled with his community on Turkey Island or Fighting Island [in the Detroit River opposite Rivière aux Canards] around July 16, 1815; around 1819 he moved to the Miami [Maumee] River (Goltz 1973: 356; Schmalz: 114; Sugden: 196, 200, 211-212; DCB vol. V: 799; MPHSC vol. XV: 492, 593, vol. XVI: 175).[117]

Wawanosh / Way-way-nosh / Joshua Wawanosh [born 1786 or 1792; died at Sarnia in 1879], head chief of the St. Clair River Ojibwa, son of

---

116 Smith, *Sacred Feathers*, 110-111. Kegedoon's great-grandson was Lawrence A. Keeshig from "Historic Sketches of Cape Croker Indians," *Canadian Echo* (Wiarton, Ontario), 8 January 1931. The Methodist William Case contended that Kegedoons had drowned, 293.

117 Curnoe, *Deeds*, 78.

Metahbick and Chief Puck-a-nonce, and grandson of an Ojibwa chief; it was stated in 1871 that Wawanosh's home territory was in the Lake Superior region, and that he ended up in Sarnia after killing a man back there. Wa-wanosh = Waving (Richardson: 101). 'Your Red Children make this request for these considerations. First, because the surrenders made to our Great Father Ostegwuum [Sir Francis Bond Head] was made through fear and not voluntary; as we are prepared to prove. Second, Because the persons who made the surrender had no power or authority to do so, but acted in direct opposition to the decision of a Grand Council held at Munsey Town in 1835 that lodged a document in the hands of our late Father Sir John Colborne deciding that no person or persons shall have any authority to sell or surrender the Saugeen lands except in Grand Council of Ojibway chiefs and not even in such council until Wawanosh [White Elk] the head chief of the tribe shall give his consent'—1838.[118]

Maticwaub/The Bow, sketched by Paul Kane at Saugeen, 1845. "I sketched the principle chief, named Maticwaub, or 'The Bow.' The band of which he is the head chief forms a part of the great nation of the Ojibbeways, which still inhabits the shores of Lake Huron, Michigan and Superior." [119]

Maskuhnoonjee/Big Pike, sketched by Paul Kane at Saugeen, 1845. I also took a sketch of a chief named Maskuhnoonjee, or 'the Big Pike.' This man was very proud of having his likeness taken, and put on his chief's medal presented by the Government to those they acknowledge as chiefs. I have never known a chief to barter away one of these marks of distinction, which they seldom wear on unimportant occasions."[120]

Wahpus/ The Rabbit, sketched by Paul Kane at Saugeen, 1845. "Wahpus, 'the Rabbit,' also permitted me to take his portrait. He resides at Owen's Sound, and was formerly as much renowned for his unconquerable fierceness and intemperance as he is now for his temperance and wisdom. This change in character is attributable to the Methodist missionaries, whose church he has joined. He was the first Indian I had seen whose hair had been pulled out, all except the scalp-lock; this custom is common amongst many tribes of Indians, though not universal amongst any.[121]

---

118 Ibid. 157-158.

119 Kane, *Wanderings*, 4.

120 Ibid. 5.

121 Ibid.

APPENDIX 8

The Great Wampum Belt of the Six Nations[122]

Chief Yellowhead rose up and made a speech and exhibited the great Wampum belt of the Six Nations, and explained the talk contained in it…

John S. Johnston, one of the Mohawk chiefs, next addressed the council… Johnston then explained the emblems contained in the wampum belt brought by Yellowhead, which, he said, they acknowledged to be the acts of their fathers. Firstly, the council fire at the Sault Ste. Marie has no emblem, because then the council was held. Secondly, the council fire as Mamtoulin [sic] has the emblem of a beautiful white fish; this signifies purity, or a clean white heart—that all our hearts ought to be white toward each other. Thirdly, the emblem of a beaver, placed at an island on Penetanguishew [sic] Bay, denotes wisdom—that all the acts of our fathers were done in wisdom. Fourthly, the emblem of a white deer placed at Lake Simcoe, signifies superiority; the dish and ladles at the same place signify abundance of game and food. Fifthly, the eagle perched on a tall pine tree at the Credit denotes watching, and swiftness in conveying messages. The eagle was to watch all the council fires between the Six Nations and Ojebways; [sic] and being far sighted, he might, in the event of anything happening, communicate the tidings to the different tribes. Sixthly, the sun was hung up in the centre of the belt, to show that their acts were done in the face of the sun, by whom they swore that they would forever after observe the treaties made between the two parties.

---

122 Jones Rev. Peter. History of the Ojebway Indians: With Especial Reference to their Conversion to Christianity, London: 1861, 120-122.